2/22/07

To Anne Barnett

This is a story of Europe's
dark ops in 20 Century
in late 1980's

John Ofal

I NEVER SAW MY FACE

I NEVER SAW MY FACE

Sam Goetz

Rutledge Books, Inc. Danbury, CT

ALL RIGHTS RESERVED
Rutledge Books, Inc.
107 Mill Plain Road, Danbury, CT 06811
1-800-278-8533
www.rutledgebooks.com

Manufactured in the United States of America

Cataloging in Publication Data
Goetz, Samuel
    I Never Saw My Face

    ISBN: 1-58244-136-7

    1. Goetz, Samuel. 2. Shoah -- World War II. 3. Holocaust --
Survivor -- Biography. 4. Poland -- Biography.

Library of Congress Catalog Card Number: 2001086396

To the Past: To my Parents,

Eugenia Gutwirt Goetz and Joseph Goetz

To the Present: My wife *Gerti*

My Children: *Joseph and Eugenia (Genie)*

My Grandchildren: *Alexa, Justin, Nathaniel, Hannah, Emily, Daniel and Aaron*

and to all children who were oppressed in Nazi occupied Europe.

ACKNOWLEDGEMENTS

I owe words of special appreciation to those who provided me with the encouragement to write *I Never Saw My Face*.

To my wife, Gerti, who first heard the story of my miraculous survival fifty-five years ago on a beach in Southern Italy and who heard the accounts many more times.

To my friends Ora and Arnold Band who travelled with me and my wife to Poland, and who revisited some of the places which are described in the book.

To my friend Florabel Kinsler, who encouraged me to write the story.

Special thanks to historians; Saul Friedlander of UCLA, Michael Berenbaum of Shoa Foundation, Marilyn Harran of Chapman University, who reviewed my manuscript.

To historian David Myers of UCLA for his sensitivity and insights in providing me with valuable advise while I was writing this difficult account of my youth in Nazi occupied Europe.

PREFACE

Why did I let so many years pass before committing my memories to writing? There are several reasons for the delay, among them the fact that even now the memories of those terrible years remain extremely painful. To summon them forth for the purpose of recording them is to restore their freshness and to relive nightmares experienced at the hands of the Nazis. For many years I found the memories of my childhood friends who, at the age of fourteen, met their deaths in the gas chambers of Belzec, and the memories of my parents who left on a cattle train to die in those same gas chambers, simply too painful to write about.

I had just turned eleven when the Germans occupied my home town and I began to experience the collapse and destruction of everything and everyone dear to me. During the occupation I witnessed, first through the eyes of a child and later through those of a hardened youth of fifteen, terrible barbarism and violence and a horrific demonstration of man's inhumanity to man. It was not easy then, in my formative years, to assimilate such events. I searched for answers, as I still do today, to such questions as: How can any "civilized" human being dispassionately murder women and children during the day, and then return home to face his own wife and play with his own children at night?

When I was liberated I found the desire to go on and rebuild my shattered life and to triumph over the sadness that had replaced the euphoria of liberation. The barbed wire, the watchtowers, the lice, the hunger and the beatings were consigned to the realm of nightmares and memories. The first few months after liberation were devoted to regaining the body mass I had lost during captivity; I quickly added thirty pounds to my liberated weight of less than eighty! In the first few months after the war there existed a form of denial, according to which survivors in the DP camps seldom talked to each other about death and concentration camps, but focussed instead on the search for loved ones and their hopes for the future.

My experiences in Italy were regenerating: the warm sun, the ocean and the clear blue skies provided a perfect backdrop against which to restore the harmony of body, mind and soul. In this idyllic setting memories of the immediate past were overwhelmed by the simple rediscovery of life. I had never before known large cities like Naples and Rome, and I became fascinated by just watching the simple events of normal daily life unfold within them. In the streets and cafes of these ancient Italian cities I experienced a zest for life that helped suppress the painful memories.

Santa Maria had enabled me to heal myself, at least superficially, and to regain the sense of self which had been stolen from me and replaced by a number in the concentration camp. Now it was time for me to build a life, to wrest back the education which had been abruptly curtailed when I was eleven. On the beach in Santa Maria I met a thirteen-year-old girl (later to become my wife) who was attending an Italian high school, and I became fascinated with the subjects she was studying.

Once in America, work and school, the building of a new life consumed my energies. The future was opening up and it claimed priority over the past which now seemed to surface only occasionally in the form of nightmarish dreams. However, after having seemingly reestablished normal life with a growing family, the search for a "relaxing" vacation took me back to Europe. This visit rekindled the past, and both bad memories and good combined to produce a bittersweet experience. In Italy, happy memories surged to the fore, but then in Austria, my wife's birthplace and the scene of my own concentration camp experience in Mauthausen-Ebensee, the darkness returned and the painful memories flooded in.

The 1970s and 1980s saw the rise of a new breed of political extremist bent on denying that the events of the Holocaust has ever occurred. My wartime memories surged forward, blended with a furious anger at the revisionist lies: Where then were our parents, our grandparents, our children and our friends? The desire to write these memories began to crystallize in my mind. I wanted my children and grandchildren to learn what had happened to their grandparents and great-grandparents. I felt they needed to understand that the world is far from perfect, and that they must shoulder the burden of safeguarding their children and ensure that a better, more humane civilization can arise out of the wreckage of their ancestors' past.

In addition, I wished to address several questions that have been posed to me in the course of my journey from liberation to the present. I am frequently asked, quite simply: How did I survive? I naturally have, thought about this many times and the only answer I can give is that a particular set of circumstances allowed me to slip through the cracks of the Nazi killing machine.

Another question is: Do I hate the Germans? I have often considered this question, too, and, after searching my feelings, I do have to admit that while visiting Germany, when I saw an elderly German the thought would pass through my mind that he could have been "one of them." This would arouse my anger, but I harbor no collective hatred against "the Germans" as a whole.

I am also frequently asked about my belief in God in the light of my Holocaust experiences. I must admit I have been unable to come to terms with this question. At the same time I must also concede that at the height of the deportations to the extermination camps I had several experiences that might be called spiritual—two of which saved me from certain death. I often think about these experiences.

The question also arises as to whether I have been able to attach any broader meaning to my survival. Why did I survive when most of my family and my young classmates perished in the gas chambers of Belzec, or survived the deportations only to later lose their lives in the concentration camps? Is there any meaning to my own survival? I have no answer to this question, unless it be simply that Providence wished me to live.

Part One

Europe

CHAPTER 1

Early Childhood
(1928 - 1939)

In the summer of 1985 I decided to revisit my hometown of Tarnow in Poland, forty-two years after I left the city on the way to a Nazi concentration camp. I was aware that the trip would be full of emotional ups and downs and bittersweet memories of a lost childhood and the loss of my parents. Thus with trepidation I boarded the plane with my wife, Gerti, and our friends, Ora and Arnold Band, that would take us to Warsaw.

We spent two days in Warsaw and then engaged a Polish driver to take us to Tarnow via Krakow. After a six-hour drive through the Polish countryside, we arrived in Krakow—a city that held particular memories for me for I spent nine months in Krakow-Plaszow concentration camp. The town had been spared destruction during the war and the cathedral and Wawel castle stood majestically in the center of the town. We traveled on to Tarnow, which is located about fifty miles east of Krakow, passing small towns and villages that I recalled from my childhood. As the car approached the city outskirts, I recognized the rolling hills, which I had visited as a child.

Tarnow is located in the foothills of the Carpathian mountains in southwestern Poland. The mountains lay to the south with St.

Martin's peak visible from the town's center, the Rynek. The winter preceding my birth had been an extremely harsh one during which hungry wolves had appeared at the foot of St. Martin's in search of prey. To the other side of Tarnow stretched an expanse of wheat fields which, in spring, is dotted with red poppies and cornflowers.

I was born on June 8, 1928 in an apartment of a three-story house on Asnyka 1, in a mixed neighborhood of Jews and Catholics. Tarnow, including the industrial suburb of Moscice, had a population of about sixty-five thousand, of whom approximately half were Jews. There was one streetcar—a concession to modern times. Its route followed the town's three main streets: Krakowska, Walowa, and Lwowska. Krakowska was the most prosperous thoroughfare, lined with sidewalk cafes, nice stores, modern apartment houses, and two movie houses. It was in this district that the well-to-do Catholic and Jewish Poles lived—middle-class Jews who were shopkeepers, merchants, and small businessmen, and a small number of nouveau rich mill owners, bankers, and industrialists who had aspirations to be acculturated. Emancipated, they often spoke Polish at home and tended to emulate their Polish acquaintances. There was also a small group of professionals—doctors, lawyers, and gymnasium professors.

As the streetcar made a sharp turn into Walowa Street, the surroundings began to change; delicatessens and leather goods stores lined the street, predominantly owned by Jews who also lived in the neighborhood. Finally, as the car entered Lwowska Street; the houses became smaller as the streetcar proceeded east, crossing the narrow streets and winding alleys that intersected Lwowska. Here, in what was the Jewish section of town, lived the poorer Jews of Tarnow and most of the Orthodox Jews. The destitute would knock on the doors of the more affluent Jews every Friday before the Sabbath begging for alms. When asked who was at the door, they would reply *"Biedny"* ("the poor"). The Orthodox children attended *cheder*, knew little Polish, and spoke mostly Yiddish. Their fine silk garb distinguished them from their poorer coreligionists. On Friday evening and on the Sabbath, these Orthodox Jews, clad in their traditional black *kapotes* (garment) and large fur hats, attended their neighborhood synagogue.

My parents, in their late twenties when I was born, aspired to a modern identity. My father usually wore a suit and a tie and my mother dressed according to current fashions. They spoke Polish to my elder brother, Bernard, and me, although my mother spoke Yiddish to her mother. On High Holidays Bernard and I accompanied them to the new synagogue, built in 1908 and dedicated on Kaiser Franz Joseph's birthday in 1908. It was a massive structure with a large cupola visible from many parts of the town. The interior had large columns and the seats were made out of stone.

My father was short with a light complexion, blue eyes, and tremendous energy. He was a jovial man, often humming tunes from Viennese operas he had often heard as a young man when our part of Poland was still part of Austria. With his mother-in-law as his partner, my father imported rabbit skins, which were cut and dyed for fur coats and exported under the company name *Polskin*. The skins were called sealskins and were quite popular and less expensive than the prestigious Persian Mantels worn by the rich Jews of Tarnow. The Persian Mantels were made of lambskin and embellished with foxtails. Wearing them, the ladies felt they had "arrived."

In the course of his business my father traveled frequently and his trips to other countries brought me much joy for he would always bring me back gifts: stamps from Belgium, a stamp catalog from Leipzig, or a watch from Czechoslovakia. On the weekend, whenever he was in town, I accompanied my father to my maternal grandmother's house where a room with a telephone served as his office. In the back of the house a German shepherd dog named Aza barked viciously if anyone approached the house, providing protection for my grandmother who lived alone.

My mother was a very pretty woman. She was about five-foot-two-inches tall, dark-haired, and reasonably slim by European standards. Her green eyes revealed both beauty and a certain melancholy. She did not participate in the business, spending her time bringing up Bernard and me. Bernard, seven years my senior, was a sickly child afflicted with croup. His poor health took a great toll on my mother, who traveled with him to various medical specialists. By the age of seven, however, soon after I was born, Bernard overcame his childhood ailment. He joined a Zionist organization, *Akiba*, and, during the summer months, he spent his time in camps sponsored by that group. My parents decided my brother should attend a Polish public high school, a decision that placed Bernard in a class where only two or three students were Jewish. He often complained at home about the anti-Jewish remarks made to him by his classmates and he was frequently teased about being Jewish and, on several occasions, harassed after school. Nevertheless, my parents decided he should remain at the public school.

Also living with us was my Polish Catholic nanny, Tekla, who came to our household soon after I was born. As my mother was unable to produce milk to feed me, and Tekla had a child at the same time, she was hired as my wet-nurse. Tekla's son, Bronek, was left with a peasant family and she stayed on in our home as my nanny. Tekla had a wrinkled face, often went barefoot, always wore a babushka on her head, and cared for me with kindness and warmth as I grew up. This uneducated woman, who was unable to read, took me to the public library where, at an early age, I discovered the pleasure of reading. She also helped my brother on one occasion. When my brother was accosted upon leaving school, Tekla, who had been hiding around a corner, chased his tormentors away while swinging a broomstick at them.

When I turned six our family moved into a modern four-story building on Pilsudski Street in the same middle-class neighborhood as the house in which I was born. The community was mixed with Jews and Catholics sharing the neighborhood stores and the Bank of Poland, located just across the street from our new residence. There was great excitement when our new neighbors obtained a motion picture camera. With a large white sheet draped over a door, they showed a Western movie for all the neighborhood kids. We eagerly gathered in their apartment to see this sensational film of horses and cowboys, thrilled at the images running across the white sheet.

Unlike my brother, I attended a private school, *Safah Berura* (Clear Language). It was a secular school with a Zionist emphasis and provided classes through the sixth grade. Classes started at eight in the morning and lasted until two o'clock. Even in winter I walked to school, sometimes through a foot of snow. I learned Hebrew and Polish, Polish history, literature, and mathematics. The president, Mr. Lieblich, was also the director of a Jewish orphanage located in a poor section of the city and some of the children from the orphanage also attended the school, apparently on scholarships.

In 1935 the Polish marshall, Joseph Pilsudski, who had led Poland since its independence in 1918, died. I was in the first grade and our teacher, Mrs. Rosner, urged the kids in my class to write letters of condolences to the Polish government offices. She also said the best letter writer was to be rewarded with a new bicycle but no child in my school received such a prize.

The Polish winter began in November when the first snow fell and, as the snow became more plentiful, I joined my friends, Moniek Rinder and Edek Dar, after school in a nearby park where we went sleigh riding down the little hill. When I reached the age of eight I received my first pair of skis. I waxed the bottom of the skis to provide an easy ride, which was soon interrupted with many falls. I learned how to ice skate soon after and, during the winter months, my classmates and I would go ice-skating in the park. Again, after many falls, I finally learned how to sail on the ice.

The winter continued until the end of April when the sun melt-
ed the snow and small patches of fresh grass emerged. With the
smell of spring in the air, the month of May was welcomed with
great excitement as we children anticipated the summer months.
When I finished the fifth grade, in June of 1939, and as I had
achieved good grades, my father rewarded me with a watch and a
Boy-Scout knife with a green handle. My parents arranged for me
to spend two months in a summer camp at Rabka, near the
Czech-Polish border in the foothills of the Tatra Mountains. I proudly took my new knife along to the summer camp. I was excited
about hiking in the woods, marching to and scaling the nearby hills,
and building dams in local streams. I gathered mushrooms in a
nearby forest and caught butterflies in the meadows where the
smell of wildflowers and green grass added to the joy of the daily
excursions. My mother was unable to visit for she had undergone
major surgery to remove a cyst from her ovaries and was spending
the last two summer months of 1939 in the Czech resort of
Zugmantel recuperating. My father was able to visit me now and
then for a few days and I looked forward to his visits and our walks
in the woods.

On August 20, 1939 my father suddenly appeared in Rabka to
take me home. He told me that war might break out and so he wanted me to be home. I said goodbye to my fellow campers and left
Rabka with sadness to board the train back to Tarnow. I stood on the
back platform of the railroad car where there was an open space. I
looked with pleasure at the mountains and forests surrounding this
pretty little town; I had a feeling I might not see this place again. It
was not until our train stopped at Tarnow and my father and I left
the station that I noticed machine-gun nests on the roofs of the tall
buildings around the railway station. There were soldiers milling
around, people rushing toward the station, and I could sense the
tension in the air.

Over the next few days my classmates also began to return to Tarnow. I met Moniek and another friend, Leszek Neuman, and we talked about our summer vacation. My parents discussed the possibility of war; the names of Daladier, Chamberlain, Hitler and Beck, the Polish foreign minister, were mentioned at the dinner table. They anxiously awaited the daily newspaper and on Monday, August 26, my parents, my brother, and I lined up to obtain gas masks and a carpenter reinforced our windows with plywood shutters.

On Friday, September 1, I awoke at dawn. It was still dark and our windows, covered with plywood and reinforced with tape, allowed very little light through. In the distance I heard loud explosions. Tarnow and its suburbs were being bombed. My parents turned on the Philips radio, which blared out Polish patriotic music, interrupted by an announcer who hailed the heroic Polish resistance to the German army's onslaught. I did not comprehend the gravity of what was happening. Certainly, I did not know at that moment that my life would never again be the same.

From the first to the seventh of September, Tarnow was suspended in a twilight zone where chaos and lawlessness reigned. Our neighbors began to pack up. My friend, Ignatz Pomerantz, who lived in the same house as we did, left with his parents. I watched as his family belongings were placed on a horse-drawn buggy and took off toward Iwowska Street, which led toward the eastern part of Poland. The banks opened for only a few hours and people wandered about in the streets. Children, including myself, were thrilled to watch the dogfights overhead, often mistakenly cheering when a plane was shot down, realizing too late it was a Polish and not a German plane that had crashed to the ground.

The news on Polish radio was contradictory, speaking of heroic resistance and Polish counterattacks, but it soon became obvious the German forces were penetrating deeper into Polish territory.

More of our neighbors left Tarnow and the streets leading east were clogged with people fleeing from the German army. My brother, Bernard, who was now eighteen, decided to leave as well, joining a Polish army unit and leaving with a small contingent of soldiers. The Polish authorities left Tarnow on Thursday, September 6. The next day, I ventured out into the street with my father, who had refused to flee east with my brother. It was a clear, sunny day. The streets of Tarnow were empty as we left our house on Pilsudski Street and made our way toward Walowa Street, the main thoroughfare leading east. The city possessed a ghostly atmosphere and a frightening silence prevailed as the two of us stood on the sidewalk, expecting the Nazi army to appear at any time. My father did not display any fear; perhaps the fact that he had dealt with German businessmen provided him with a false sense of security. Having read about wars during the Middle Ages and World War I, I had only a romanticized vision of heroic battles, making me more curious than fearful about the soldiers that were going to enter Tarnow at any moment.

At about eleven o'clock a sound of engines broke through the air. The first tank with a large Nazi emblem on it turned into Walowa Street, soon followed by other tanks with their guns protruding menacingly. German soldiers in full combat gear marched along the sidewalk, staying close to the walls for protection from possible sniper fire. Some of the tanks turned toward the town's main square, the Rynek. There, the tank soldiers emerged from their vehicles. As I stood there motionless, I marveled at the extraordinary sight. I certainly had no idea the world was on the verge of being plunged into darkness.

CHAPTER 2

Living on the Edge
(1939 - 1941)

The month of September 1939 changed my life forever. The chief administrator of the German occupation regime of Tarnow was *Kreishauptman* Ernst Kundt and Tarnow's Jews quickly became familiar with his name and his endless stream of anti-Jewish decrees. Jewish businesses were taken over by German administrators and Jewish merchandise was confiscated. During the first few days of occupation the Nazis sought out prominent Jewish citizens, rounded them up as hostages and executed them. Placards announcing new German edicts, signed by Kundt, appeared almost daily. A seven o'clock curfew was imposed and became a source of tension in our home. As the hour approached, the streets became deserted, the silence interrupted only by the heavy thuds of the boots of German patrols. My father often tested the patrols' resolve by returning home a few minutes after seven. All Jews over the age of six had to wear white armbands, ten centimeters wide, with the Star of David on them. Anyone found without the star would be shot immediately. Overnight, a temporary armband-sewing industry sprung up and I found myself wearing what my ancestors wore in the Middle Ages. With the star visible from a distance, the Jews of Tarnow became more vulnerable to assaults by local Nazis, hooligans, and German troops passing through on their way toward the eastern part of occupied Poland.

Because of acute shortages of butter, milk, sugar, meat, and other staples, food rationing was introduced. Outlying farms had orders to deliver the bulk of their produce to the occupation forces. People lined up as early as four-thirty a.m. to obtain the meager daily bread ration and a black market developed to sell this and other precious commodities. Tekla, who was still living with us, was able to get us a little milk, bread, and marmalade, so I did not suffer from hunger.

At the end of the year, Kundt issued a proclamation that all Jews were to bring their valuables, including fur coats, jewelry, gold, silver, and foreign currency, to the German town council. Any violation would be punished by death. My mother and father sold their fur coats to our Polish acquaintances to avoid giving them to the Germans. At the same time, a census of livable apartments took place as German civilians and officers were to be placed with Jewish families. Fortunately we escaped this ordeal, although some of our furniture was requisitioned for the newly arriving occupation forces.

The winter of 1939 was approaching fast. Jewish children were prohibited from attending Polish schools and so, at the end of November my mother, along with some friends, decided that schooling should be continued at home. Several of my friends' parents offered their apartments and we rotated the location for the lessons. Giving lessons was a dangerous undertaking and especially so in our apartment building as several Nazi officials resided there. Thus, each lesson was accompanied with a fear of being discovered and, while walking on the street, books had to be camouflaged. The teachers were the former instructors from my Hebrew school and the Jewish high school who had not already left Tarnow. Middle-aged, they risked their lives daily to help us continue our education.

They tried to follow the old *Gymnasium*, or high school curriculum, offering Polish grammar, German gothic script, Old Latin, and algebra. I also continued English lessons with Mr. Wrubel, a man in his early fifties who had lived in the United States for nine years. I learned and memorized English grammar and, as I progressed, he introduced me to English short stories.

Collecting stamps became my pastime. I collected all the new stamps that the Nazis issued. I even subscribed to the German Philatelic Service located in Krakow and had stamps sent to me COD. It was such a joy when the mailman delivered these new stamps to the house and collected the money from my mother. Some days, without my parents' knowledge, I would remove my Star of David armband, go to the post office and purchase the latest German stamps with the official Nazi stamp on the envelope. All black market activities, such as running over to the German post office and removing the Star of David in order to purchase new German *Winterhilfe* stamps, were extremely dangerous. But, as a twelve-year-old, I hardly realized how dangerous.

Early in December the streets of Tarnow were covered with a blanket of snow and the days were short, with darkness falling around four o'clock. One Friday evening, my mother invited a neighbor's son, Heniek Krants, for evening supper. Although his father and two brothers lived in America, the family of three that remained in Tarnow was very poor and my mother frequently invited Heniek to our house for something to eat. Heniek, who was several years my senior, would play chess with me or we would play cards.

It was about seven-thirty in the evening when Heniek left our apartment on his way home. He was hardly out of the door when, suddenly, I heard loud screams and a loud banging on our front door. Heniek rushed in, followed by uniformed Nazis and several civilians wearing swastika armbands. Loud screams of "*Juden raus!"* ("Jews out!") reverberated around our home and in the corridors of the apartment building. One of the Nazis took out a revolver and placed it against my temple. I felt the cold steel on my face. Seconds later, I found myself, along with my parents, on the street. It was a clear, cold night and on the horizon a red glow illuminated the sky. Not far from Pilsudski Street the main Tarnow synagogue was on fire. As my parents and I made our way to the apartment of my mother's younger brother, stunned and frightened by the screams of the wild, unruly mob, the fire and the glow became more visible. We spent the "night of the burning synagogues" with my Uncle Willek Gutwirt, his wife and their two small children, shaken up by this frightening experience. The main Tarnow synagogue continued to burn and finally the remnants of the building that had taken so many years to build was blown up.

The next day, Saturday, we returned to our apartment on Pilsudski Street. The apartment was intact; nothing had been taken away in spite of the fact that, following our violent expulsion, the door had remained unlocked. My parents and I remained in shock. We were frightened, not knowing what would happen next. The curiosity I had felt while waiting for the German soldiers to enter Tarnow three months earlier had disappeared and the reality of war and our German occupiers now frightened me.

By mid-December definite borders were established between the western, German- occupied part of Poland, and the eastern, Soviet-occupied region. Many families were now permanently sundered; fathers and sons found themselves separated from their wives and mothers. A new art of smuggling people across the San River, back to German-occupied territory, became the province of skilled Polish smugglers. The cost was high and there were no guarantees of safe passage. My parents had not received any communication from my brother, Bernard, although in early January 1940 refugees returning to Tarnow claimed to have spotted him alive in the city of Lwow. My mother contacted a well-known smuggler in Tarnow and paid him to find her eldest son in Lwow and bring him home across the border. We waited for news but for the next few weeks no information reached us about the smuggling efforts. My daily occupation became the interception of the mailman in search of a letter from my brother. Finally, in early February 1940, a large envelope, bearing colorful Russian stamps, appeared. I ran to the house quickly and my mother began to read the letter. Her face paled. My brother wrote he would soon be reunited with us. Our hearts sank for the letter had been mailed three weeks earlier. Something clearly had gone wrong. We contacted the smuggler and soon discovered that Bernard, along with others, had been caught at the river crossing, arrested by the Soviets, and deported to the interior of the Soviet Union.

In the early spring of 1940 we had visitors: a blue-uniformed, Polish police officer who was accompanied by a uniformed Nazi. At first, my mother and I were apprehensive but we soon learned the man was an acquaintance of my father's from Germany. His name was Steinweiler and he had come to Tarnow from Leipzig to see my father. My father and Steinweiler, in his brown SA uniform, talked for many hours. He had come to help us, but there was not really much he could do. Soon after his visit, however, some of our furniture, previously requisitioned, was returned to us.

Gestapo agents arrived in Tarnow with the task of "resolving the Jewish problem." I became familiar with the names of the Gestapo agents such as von Malotke, who struck terror in the hearts of Jews. Soon, other names became part of our daily vocabulary: Novak, Rommelman, Kastura. Many Jews now began to be arrested. People were picked up by the Gestapo or the *Kripo* (criminal police) for alleged violations of black market regulations, such as the possession of foreign currency. The *Kripo* would drive around in yellow Volkswagens, speeding through the narrow streets and screeching to a halt to pick up their victims. Those arrested would never be seen again.

Early in May, as I was crossing a small park on my way to my clandestine lessons, a German soldier stopped me. Despite my attempts to explain to this soldier that I needed to be someplace, he took me to the German army barracks on the outskirts of town, saying that *"Die Truppe geht vort"* ("The army is more important"). At the barracks I was ordered to clean the latrines. Given a pail of water and a brush I spent all day cleaning the filthy latrines. With no means of notifying my parents, and given no food, I worked in the barracks until late in the evening. Finally, I was allowed to go home to my anxious parents.

In the late spring the *Judenrat* (Jewish Council) and the *Ordnungsdienst* (Jewish police force) were formed. Clad in hats bearing the Jewish star and given wooden batons, the *Ordnungsdienst* became the tool of the *Judenrat*. The council consisted of twelve members from the Jewish community. Its function was to implement orders from the Gestapo and other German agencies that dealt with the Jews. In many instances the *Judenrat* was the only place to which Jews could turn to try to obtain the release of a loved one from a labor camp or jail. But, subjected to pressure from the Gestapo, the function of the council changed as the measures against the Jewish population grew harsher. The council now had to implement many new orders and requests from the Gestapo, the Nazi civilian administration, and often the German army. Thus, requests for slave labor, goods, and the arrests of Jews were often the preoccupation of Jewish council members. Members of the council became the new "elite" of the Jewish community and were viewed by the rest of the Jews of Tarnow with mixed feelings. Granted certain deceptive privileges, they labored under the illusion that they were exempt from the harsh anti-Jewish measures. And, as the anti-Jewish actions and arrests continued, the Jews began to view the council in Tarnow as a powerless institution.

September 1940 marked the end of the first year of Nazi occupation. There was uncertainty about the future and anxiety about the coming winter months. As the days became shorter, the darkness and the early curfew imposed additional hardships on an already depressed Jewish population. Sometime in early October, my father and I were returning to our apartment on Pilsudski Street after visiting my grandmother. It was already dark, and we were rushing home to beat the curfew. About a block from our apartment house, on the corner of our street, stood a German policeman. In his green uniform he looked like a beast, a creature awaiting its prey. We sensed danger. Our armbands were clearly in sight. The policeman approached. Throwing away his cigarette he stood with clenched fists about a foot away from us. Instinctively, my father removed his hat as a gesture of respect for a Nazi officer. The policeman stopped suddenly in front of us and with a hateful expression and a terse voice, muttered *"Du hast Gluck, Jude"* ("You are lucky, Jew"). Frightened and deeply shaken by this experience we finally reached the door of our apartment, feeling helpless and humiliated.

Not far from our apartment, the Germans established the city's administrative office, the *Kreishauptmannschaft*. After the early morning lessons I would get together with two friends from my old school, *Safa Berura:* Abras Koch, whose parents had a textile store presently taken over by Nazi trustees, and Tulek Siedliskier. Tulek's father was in the Soviet sector of Poland and Tulek and his mother and sister waited anxiously for any word from him. But there was no news about his father and he never did return to Tarnow. The three of us would walk the streets of the Jewish section of Tarnow, hoping to meet the girls from *Safa Berura*. Sometimes, my friends would accompany me to the German post office, where all three of us would enter without our Jewish armbands.

Once a week, I accompanied my mother when she visited Mrs. Roskies who lived in a pleasant section of Tarnow, just off Krakowska Street. Mrs. Roskies addressed my mother's letters to my brother in Russian. The visits to Mrs. Roskies were always sad for me. My mother worried terribly about my brother in Russia, opening her heart to Mrs. Roskies about her fears. Once addressed, the letters were sent to Kandalaksha, on the Cola peninsula in the region of Murmansk where Bernard was serving a sentence for his attempt to smuggle himself back home to Tarnow. Bernard survived the war and finally came to the U.S. in 1973. My mother also prepared packages to be sent via our cousin, Helen Handgriff, who lived in the Russian part of Poland. Helen, who had escaped from Tarnow in 1939, married her fiancé, and now lived in Brzezany, not far from the city of Lwow.

The streets of Tarnow were covered with snow. The ice-skating rink behind our apartment building was now closed to Jewish children and my friends and I greatly missed our ice-skating. I stood at the window, trying to catch a glimpse of the Polish children skating on the ice. As the winter weather got worse, I was confined more and more to the apartment. There were shortages of coal and staple foods and, to make ends meet, my father decided to sell one of his watches, a thin, Swiss-made gold watch that had been a wedding gift. One afternoon in December 1940, I accompanied my father on a visit to some Polish acquaintances who bought the watch that I had often admired. It must have been painful for my father to part with his watch, but he said nothing to me.

My morning lessons became less regular because several teachers had difficulties of their own and could not always come to the lessons. Some afternoons, particularly on Saturdays, I went with my parents to my father's office in my grandmother's house in the Jewish section of town. My father could not continue his business since trading in furs was forbidden to Jews and all fur coats had to

Sam's parents.
Picture taken circa early 1918.
Sam's father in an Austrian Army uniform.

Sam's family—Poland, 1938. **From left:** Sam, age 10;
his brother Bernard, age 17; his mother, age 39;
and his father, age 39.

Apartment house in
Tarnow, Poland.
Lower floor is
where Sam was
born.

Four story house in the center of Tarnow, Poland.
Where Sam lived from 1935 to 1940.

Main Street, Tarnow, Poland. Where Sam witnessed
the German army entering Tarnow on
September 7, 1939.

Tekla Nagorska—a
Tarnow Polish Catholic
nanny who saved
Sam's life in WW II.
Picture taken in 1946.

Tekla Nagorska.
In the back-
ground is the
house where
Sam lived from
1935 to 1940.

The Rynek—or city main square—where many Jewish stores were located. It was used as a killing area of Jews in June, 1942.

Tarnow. The interior of the main synagogue
blown up by the Nazis in December, 1939.

The main synagogue in Tarnow.
Burned in December, 1939.

Tarnow. Charred remnants of a
burned out 19th century synagogue.
It was destroyed in December, 1939.

be turned over to the German authorities. My father still had some skins, hidden in Krakow, that he sold on the black market in spite of the fact this was punishable by death.

The winter of 1940 was bitterly cold. Lack of proper heating aggravated the situation and many Jewish families in Tarnow froze. Coal, the main source of fuel, was rationed and the Polish Catholics received a larger allotment while the Jews were allocated very little coal. The view of snow and ice, which in normal times would have been a pastoral scene, now caused anxiety, since we were short of any heating material. Occasionally, a letter would arrive from my brother in Russia. It would be mailed to my cousin, Helen, in Brzezany, who would forward it to us in Tarnow, as my brother could not write to us directly from the Russian camp. His letters described the harsh winter in the Murmansk region—the white nights and the loss of night vision due to a lack of vitamin A. My father tried to console my mother that the port of Murmansk does not freeze, since it is located on the Gulf Stream, which acts as a warming influence. I became very interested in the geography of that northern region, looking it up on the map of the Soviet Union and calculating the distance in kilometers from Tarnow.

In the early months of 1941 I became violently ill. A family friend, Dr. Wachtel, the son of a well-known restaurant owner in Tarnow, came to our house. I was diagnosed with scarlet fever and was confined to bed for three weeks. Tekla brought books from the library and I devoured the ten volumes of Jean Christopher, not understanding everything, as well as novels by Leblanc, James Curwood, and Karl May.

As I was recovering, word reached us from the *Judenrat* that we had three days to vacate our apartment as it was to be taken over by a German police officer. Jews were forbidden to live in certain parts of town that were occupied by German military and civilian administration so my father found a place on Urwana Street, a one-way street in the rural outskirts of Tarnow. On Urwana Street Polish Catholics and Jews still lived on the same street. Our landlord was a Polish railroad worker and our neighbors were a Polish Catholic family, named Wozny, and a Jewish family, named Wahl. The Wozny family, who had been evicted from Poznan, had a two-year-old child and the father worked for the German railroad. The Wahls were from Kracow and had twin boys, Artek and Bronek, who were two years older than I. Tall, blond, with blue eyes, they easily blended with the population outside the ghetto walls. They were fun to be with and we soon became friends.

The move from Pilsudski Street to our new apartment on Urwana Street was painful for my parents. Most of our furniture did not fit into the small apartment and so my parents had to give it away. Tekla had to find a place of her own to live because new decrees made it illegal for Jews to have Christians working in their homes. She still arrived at our apartment on Urwana Street every morning, however, to bring us fresh bread and milk, purchased on the black market, and to help us with errands. As a Polish Catholic she was free to travel the streets of Tarnow.

Spring arrived early in Tarnow in 1941. The window of my little room looked out onto St. Martin's mountain, the edge of a forest, and the railroad tracks leading east toward Lwow. As I watched the snow melting on the mountain I recalled the excursions and summer picnics I had enjoyed with my parents before the outbreak of war. I welcomed the melting snow in April 1941 and the warmer weather.

My daily life of frequently interrupted lessons and trips to the post office to collect the new German stamps with Tulek and Abras now included preparations for my Bar Mitzvah, which was to be held on Saturday, June 21. Mr. Glass, a Hebrew teacher with a red beard, came to our apartment to prepare me for the reading of my Haftora. The celebration of Bar Mitzvah, along with any form of praying and congregating, was forbidden and, if discovered, punishable by death. Nevertheless, my parents felt that I should not miss this Jewish tradition.

As I kept busy with my Hebrew and Haftora lessons, my parents were preoccupied with the daily news of the war and the new regulations imposed on the Jews by the Germans. My father left early in the morning for his office at my grandmother's home and my mother often stood on our little balcony and said goodbye to him. My mother, who was often depressed because of my brother's absence, would venture out to buy food on the black market. Her pretty, black hair was beginning to turn gray and her green eyes were very sad. At the age of forty-one, my mother was aging fast.

One day in April my father brought the German Nazi newspaper, the *Krakauer Zeitung*, home with the headlines announcing the German occupation of Yugoslavia. A few days later came the news of the occupation of Belgrade. The Germans now controlled the Balkans.

On June 21, 1941, the big day finally arrived. The makeshift congregation was gathered about a mile from our apartment on Urwana Street. The service was to take place on the second floor of an old apartment house. One person was selected to keep a lookout for German police or Gestapo agents. As people crammed into the two small rooms, including many of my parents' old friends, I also spotted my father's new friends, the Reiss brothers, furriers who had been expelled from Berlin. The older Reiss, who spoke only German, was serving as a vice-president of the *Judenrat*.

My turn arrived. I stood anxiously in front of the many people who had crammed into the two small rooms and proudly recited my portion of the Haftora that described the story of the town of Jericho and, as I recited the ancient story of the conquest of Jericho by the Israelites, I forgot the imminent danger of living under German occupation. A kiddush followed, drinks were served, and my parents were congratulated. I was relieved at having delivered and read the Torah portion assigned to me.

After the last of our friends had left just after noon, I made my way home from the makeshift synagogue, carrying the many gifts I had received. There was a hardcover book in German, *Mozes*, the author of which I do not remember, given to me by one of the Reiss brothers, a picture book called *The Wonders of Nature*, and a pretty, red and black leather wallet. Later in the day I spread the gifts out on my bed. I liked *The Wonders of Nature* book and as I turned the pages my eyes caught the image of the Grand Canyon. I admired a photograph of a large crater created by a meteorite, somewhere in Arizona. It all seemed so unreal. Here I was in Tarnow, in German-occupied Poland, wearing the Star of David, not allowed to attend school, not allowed to ride a bike, not allowed to go to a park or a cinema, and I was looking at pictures of the beautiful Grand Canyon, spread out on my bed on this memorable day of June 21, 1941. Overwhelmed by these gifts, I lay on my bed contemplating each item, one by one. I opened the pages of *Mozes* and attempted to read it in German, but I soon returned to *The Wonders of Nature*.

Sunday, June 22, was a sunny, clear day. I woke up early, still excited about my Bar Mitzvah and the gifts I had received. About nine in the morning Tekla arrived at our apartment in an agitated state saying the streetcar had stopped running, and no one was on the streets. I walked over to Abras's and Tulek's houses and the three of us ventured out toward the town center. The streets were deserted. The streetcar, which went to the main section of Lwowska Street, where most of the Jews lived, had indeed stopped running, just as Tekla had said. As the three of us made our way toward the Jewish section, we noticed that hardly anyone was to be seen. Suddenly, newspaper boys appeared on the street screaming: "Buy the *Goniec Krakowski!*" The words "War against Russia" were emblazoned across the front of the Polish language Nazi newspaper. I left my two friends and hurried back home taking a newspaper with me. My father's face showed excitement about the news while my mother's silence conveyed her preoccupation about my brother's safety. My father left the apartment for my grandmother's house as there, in the Jewish section, he could find out more about the events of the day. The next day my father returned from Lwowska Street both anxious and hopeful. Tarnow was located about one hundred miles west of the front line, on the direct railroad link to Przemysl, the town that divided German-occupied Poland from the Russian part. If the Russian army moved toward Tarnow, what would happen to the Jews of Tarnow?

My interest shifted now from stamp collecting to collecting the news about the war. Excitedly, I found a map of Europe and one of Russia and began to read about the towns that the German papers proclaimed to have fallen to their victorious armies. On Thursday, June 25, there were banner headlines in the *Krakauer Zeitung* boasting of the German army's deep penetration into Soviet-occupied Polish territory. Two days later, one week after the beginning of the war against the Soviet Union, the headlines declared that German armies had crossed the Soviet frontier and that a large number of Russian prisoners had been taken into captivity. Beginning in July, the shops in the Polish section of Tarnow displayed large maps. Each map featured little swastika flags showing where the German armies were fighting. The flags were moved daily as the armies advanced. On Urwana Street, my window facing the railroad track became an observation post from which I watched the trains going east carrying both troops and tanks with the Nazi insignia.

August 7, 1941 brought more bad news from the front. The cities of Smolensk and Minsk had fallen to the Germans and a large number of Russians had been taken prisoner. Among the Jews of Tarnow any glimmer of hope evaporated. Even the optimists fell quiet. We could not believe the German victories were real. Our lives continued with a sense of foreboding as the Gestapo and *Kripo* became more active. More arrests were made. Jews were dragged from their homes in the middle of the night and others arrested during the day. Some were released badly shaken and broken; they refused to talk about their experiences. Rumors ran high in the Jewish section of town that those arrested had been tortured and warned not to reveal what had happened to them.

In October the days began to get cold, rain fell, and people were worried about the coming winter months. The *Krakauer Zeitung* forecast the imminent fall of Leningrad, which was surrounded. It was merely a matter of days before the German armies entered it in triumph. In the Jewish quarter a new industry developed. The German armies were short of brooms. Someone in the *Judenrat* approached my father to manufacture the brooms and soon after he set up a one-room brush factory in my aunt's apartment in the Jewish section. My cousins, my aunt, and the neighbors' children all worked creating these brushes and brooms. I worked too. Two pieces of wood, some horsehair and a stick created a broom. I went with him to purchase horsehair, which came from horsetails and was sold by the kilo. The brooms were delivered to a collection point where we were paid for them. Many such brush factories were set up in the Jewish section of town leading the Jews in Tarnow to speculate that now the Nazis needed us and therefore would not kill us.

In late November 1941, the *Krakauer Zeitung* reported the German armies were twenty kilometers from Moscow and the town of Vyazma had fallen. More gloom and anxiety were felt among the Jews of Tarnow. I sensed a pessimism in my parents as the arrest of Jews escalated. The Gestapo in Tarnow became much more aggressive as the German armies penetrated deeper into Russian territory. New members of the Gestapo began to appear in

Tarnow. The names of Sturmführer Rommelman and von Maloutke struck terror into the hearts of Jews. Rommelman, with his horse-drawn carriage, would enter the Jewish quarter and shoot any Jews appearing in his way. Von Maloutke, in his civilian clothes, visited the building where the *Judenrat* was located and shot Jews on his way in and out.

As western territories of occupied Poland were annexed to the Third Reich an ever-increasing number of Jews were expelled from other small towns in the surrounding area. Arriving in Tarnow, they were absorbed into the Jewish quarter. Jews now had to evacuate most parts of Tarnow and concentrate in the area of Lwowska Street where the poor Jews of Tarnow lived before the outbreak of the war. Old, dilapidated houses without modern toilet facilities now became the quarters for forty thousand Jews. Typhoid and typhus broke out frequently in these quarters and large quarantine notices appeared on the apartments where the sick lived. By the end of 1941 a Jewish ghetto was more or less established in Tarnow.

CHAPTER 3

From Deportations to Destruction
(1942 - 1945)

My parents and I still lived on Urwana Street outside of the Jewish quarter when the year of 1942 arrived. The January days were very cold and snow covered the streets of Tarnow. It was difficult to obtain coal to heat our apartment and electricity was also rationed. We began to use carbide lights, solid crystals of carbide placed in a container over water which then produced a gas that, when lit, provided light for the room.

New regulations issued in January required every Jew in Tarnow to have a new identification card to be carried at all times. This pink ID card had a picture affixed to it and included the bearer's date of birth and occupation. I received my ID card in early March. My occupation was listed as assistant furrier although I did not know what it all meant. I carried my new card everywhere. In April I was assigned to a workshop on Lwowska Street where fur linings were produced for German army coats. There was very little supervision. I arrived at work at eight o'clock in the morning, sorted out some skins, and left. I then joined Tulek and Abras to continue my lessons, which had become less regular as many of our teachers no longer showed up.

The spring of 1942 brought additional requests from the

Gestapo to the *Judenrat* to provide new labor battalions of young men. These men were sent to a labor camp near Tarnow called Pustkow where they repaired and cleaned cars and heavy army vehicles for the German army. They also erected telephone poles. The work was long and hard with little food for the workers. Some men managed to escape and return to Tarnow and then the Jewish section buzzed with terrible rumors about the gruesome conditions of overwork and beatings in the Pustkow camp. But most of the men never returned. In May I heard rumors that the Jews from Krakow were being deported. In the Jewish quarter there was tension in the air. People spoke in whispers on the street and there were other rumors circulating about some impending action against the Jews of Tarnow. I felt a sense of anxiety I could not define.

My fourteenth birthday fell on a sunny day on Monday June 8. Spring was in the air and I wandered out toward the fields, trying to catch a glimpse of flowers and green grass and feel the coming of spring and summer. At mid-morning I met Abras and Tulek and we went to visit our friend, Sianka Kleinhandler, a former classmate at *Safa Berura*. Sianka was rather short, with dark eyes and a pretty face. She knew well how to use her good looks to attract boys and she became very popular with the older boys who were in their third year of Gymnasium. We all had a crush on her. Sianka's father had a hardware store, and they lived in a second story apartment in the eastern part of Tarnow, not too far from the green fields and the little stream called Biala. So on this spring day we approached her house and whistled to let her know that we were waiting. She came down and we walked towards the fields, crossing an area where the former Polish high school stood, now a Nazi police administrative office. As we crossed the area we were surprised by a German civilian who stopped us, screaming that we should all be at work. As he yelled threats at us we ran away in fear.

Terrified by this encounter, the four of us decided to venture into the center of the Jewish section, the Rynek. This was an old marketplace where, before the war, Jewish merchants sold textiles, hardware goods and produce. Under the German occupation the black market thrived on the Rynek. As we entered the large square, there was a fervor in the air. People were agitated, talking in whispers. I suddenly noticed my mother shopping for food and I blushed since Sianka was with us.

On Tuesday, June 9, there was an increasing amount of tension among the Jews of Tarnow. On Lwowska Street I overheard rumors that large numbers of German SS units had arrived in town. The next day I awoke early. It was a spring day with blue skies, yet the tranquility of the morning was disrupted by a large placard posted in the Jewish section ordering Jews to register at designated places. I was walking on Lwowska Street, in the heart of the Jewish section, when a large crowd of people caught my attention, all moving in the direction of a school building. I followed the stream of people, not knowing where they were going or for what purpose and soon found myself in a large auditorium with many tables in it. Behind each table sat a uniformed SS man. Lines formed in front of each table, with each person holding their pink ID card. I placed myself in one of the lines, holding my card in my hand. I approached the table and the SS man looked first at me and then at my ID card. On the face of the card he put a round, blue-inked stamp with a Nazi eagle and swastika in the center. It contained the inscription, "Chief of the Police and Security Forces for the District of Krakow." I left the auditorium in search of my parents. Not finding them, I headed for our apartment on Urwana Street. My parents were at home, having had their ID cards stamped with the letter "K." We compared the two different stamps, the little "K" and the round blue-inked stamp on my card. My parents were tense and upset but were unable to grasp the significance of the two stamps.

At five a.m. the next morning, I was awakened by a loud banging on our door. Opening the door, I faced a Jewish Order Policeman whose name I knew to be Joiny. He told me to get dressed, get my ID card, and accompany him. My parents were allowed to stay in the apartment while I went with the policeman to the court in the *Judenrat* building on Folwarczna Street. There were many people sitting and milling around in the court. I was told to surrender my ID card and wait. The hours passed quickly; the sun rose on the horizon, and once again the skies were clear blue. My attention was focused on the stairs of the building leading into the courtyard. It was almost midday when I heard my name called. An official of the *Judenrat*, whom I did not know, returned my ID card to me and told me to return to my apartment. I was glad to rejoin my parents and tell them what had happened.

It was early in the afternoon when we all heard a loud banging on our door. I opened the door and was stunned to see three green uniformed Germans, two in SS uniform and one in the light uniform of the German police. They were dressed in full combat gear, with helmets on and small handguns over their shoulders. One of them had a list in his hand. He loudly called the name of Samek Goetz. I answered in German. Then he screamed at me to show him my ID card. He looked at it, returned it to me, and asked for my father and his ID card. My father appeared, holding his ID card. They told him to accompany them, and, as they left, said they would be back later for my mother. Bewildered by the experience I returned to the room where my mother sat in silence. My father had been led away and I was left alone with my mother. The two of us sat quietly in the apartment. I felt little fear at that moment. I must have been numb or too young to experience real fear. My mother, although very upset, did not cry; the shock of my father's arrest completely overwhelmed her. I glanced out of the window toward Urwana Street and noticed a horse-drawn carriage carrying several

Jewish men guarded by a group of SS men. The sound of shots punctuated the silence in our apartment.

Loud machine-gun fire could be heard until late in the evening. Urwana Street was far from the center of the Jewish community, and since it was forbidden to venture out with the curfew in force, we were quite isolated. We remained dressed all night, expecting at any moment to be picked up by the SS. Early in the morning we moved to our little balcony. The dawn arrived and it was Friday. Suddenly, as we sat watching the sunrise above the horizon, a figure appeared, as though through a fog, at the foot of our stairway. We made out my father's silhouette. He stepped into the little courtyard leading upstairs. I rubbed my eyes; was I dreaming? Was this wishful thinking? My thoughts were soon interrupted by a knock at the door. The moment of uncertainty gone, I opened the door and there stood my father, looking haggard and worn out. He removed his hat, threw it on the bed and said, *"Das war eine Gehenne"* ("I've come back from hell").

Later that morning we heard more gunfire. The SS units were collecting Jews from their homes and from their hiding places. The gunfire was heard all morning. Tekla found her way to our apartment and described the scenes of empty streets and of Jews being marched in a column toward the Jewish cemetery off Szpitalna Ulica. People attempted to hide, but to no avail. The old and young were collected and marched toward the cemetery. My father urged Tekla to go to the Jewish council building and contact Vice President Lehrhaupt, who was my father's friend, to see if he could help us in any way. Tekla hurried back to our house, agitated and hysterical. As she described the scene she had just witnessed in the *Judenrat* building tears came down her face. When she had arrived at the *Judenrat* building to contact Lehrhaupt, she had witnessed drunken Gestapo agents entering the building and shooting several members of the council, including Vice President Reiss, who, only one year earlier, had attended my Bar Mitzvah. Yet despite her description of these horrific crimes. In spite of my father's arrest and his experiences at the hands of the SS, my parents were not convinced of the accuracy of Tekla's account and assumed her story was exaggerated. Unable to face the violent reality of events, they could not believe that members of *Judenrat*, a council that had implemented the orders of the Gestapo, were now being shot by the Gestapo. It was a moment of disbelief and fear, of not knowing what to do next.

We spent the rest of Friday in the apartment. My father recounted what had happened to him from the moment he was taken away by the three SS men. He had been transported in one of the horse-drawn carts that the farmers used to haul wheat during the harvest. The three SS men continued to pick up other Jews on their list. The next stop was another house on Urwana Street. While two of the SS men went up to fetch more Jews, one remained to guard my father. As they waited, the SS man confessed to my father that he had witnessed the murder of about five hundred Jews that day, adding, *"Ich kann nicht mehr das dulden"* ("I cannot stand it anymore"). My father offered him his watch if he would only tell my mother where he was being taken but the guard refused, saying that he could not do what my father asked. Instead he and the other two SS men delivered the Jews, including my father, to an assembly place, a former high school building that was being used as an assembly place to collect and house the Jews until the trains arrived to take them away to their deaths. Here my father spent the night. During the night, bands of drunken SS men entered the building and terrorized the Jews. They lined them up against the wall and threatened them with execution. They beat them, but no shots were fired. It was a night of hell.

At dawn, my father spotted an empty soup or coffee kettle in the courtyard. He placed the kettle on a wheelbarrow and simply wheeled it out, past the sentry. In this way he escaped from the high school, and returned home. He kept repeating it had been a night of hell. He could not believe the Germans were capable of such behavior. My father, who frequently traveled to the German city of Leipzig for the annual trade show, could not comprehend the danger of Nazi Germany. His experience on Thursday night, June 11, 1942, left a terrible mark on him. I had never seen him so haggard and upset.

The following Saturday was a difficult day for my parents and me. Since this was a week of deportations, there was a special curfew for the Jewish population. With the special SS and police units assigned to gather and deport the Jews, Jews could not venture out onto the streets. We felt trapped. The SS and German police had blocked all roads out of Tarnow. From my window, I could see the German green police patrolling the route to the mountains where, in summer, my parents and I would go on picnics. The Jews of Tarnow were helpless. There was no escape, no rescue, and little hope; there was only fear and uncertainty.

The next day, June 14, there were rumors of another action on Monday. The word spread that on Monday everyone should report to his or her designated workplaces. People packed up their belongings. At six-thirty on Monday morning, we left the Urwana Street apartment and walked through the Jewish quarter to a workshop on Garbarska 5 in the eastern part of town. It was a furriers' workshop and I was assigned there as a furrier's assistant. Before the war, this section had housed tanneries and furriers' workshops and had been mostly inhabited by Jews.

Garbarska 5 was a two-story white building. Inside, on the right, was a workshop full of tables, pelts, and special sewing machines. On the left there was a black iron door and a stairway leading down to the cellar, which served as a storage area. My parents, along with a few others, entered through the black iron door into the basement storage area. The black iron door had a place for a padlock, although there was no padlock on it, it just hung open. I entered the workshop and was assigned to a table with pelts on it. I placed my ID card on the table in front of me. Some discussion ensued as to whether or not to place a padlock on the black iron door leading to the basement. People feared it would be broken down anyway and, in the end, it was decided to leave the door unlocked.

It was approximately ten in the morning when we heard the loud screams of a German patrol approaching. I pretended to work along with about fifty other men whose ID cards were all stamped with the round SS seal. The SS patrol, in full combat gear, entered the building. They moved from table to table, checking our ID cards, and then ascended to the second floor. Soon we heard screams as the women and children who were trying to hide upstairs were discovered. The SS brought them down and prepared to leave the building. One of them stopped in front of the unlocked, black iron door. He called his comrades' attention to it. The SS man did not go down the stairs, he simply shouted for the people in the basement to come up. With his small machine gun, he motioned for them to line up.

Through the open door I tried to catch a glimpse of my parents as they came up the stairs and through the black iron door. For a second only, I spotted my father wearing a light trench coat. As he passed through the door, he stumbled on a pail of water and then joined the others. His face seemed tense and resigned rather than fearful. This was the last time I saw my father. I missed my mother as she joined the others in the courtyard where they were assembled before moving on to the railway station. Little did I know this was the last Monday I would ever be with her. Who could have predicted that within one week, one-third of the Tarnow Jews would either be murdered in Tarnow or deported to Belzec? I had just turned fourteen; my father and my mother were both forty-three years old. The day will remain with me as long as I live, etched in stone in my memory. The abrupt separation, the brutality of not even being able to say goodbye, or share a goodbye kiss, has haunted me all these years.

The SS patrols continued their sweep of the Jewish neighborhood. Gunfire could be heard. Around one o'clock, word spread that the patrol had left the area. I draped a few pieces of fur over my arm and, leaving the building, headed down Lwowska Street. Numb and bewildered, I made my way in the direction of the other furriers' workshop. The skins served as my security blanket. I believed they, along with my ID card, would protect me. I was bewildered by what had happened, and I wanted to find out where my parents were being taken. My eyes caught the tail end of a large column of Jews being marched toward the railway station. I tried hard to catch a glimpse of my parents, but to no avail. At the rear of the column, SS men were making sure that no one escaped.

As I walked, I saw several SS men torturing a Hasidic Jew who had not shaved off his beard. Several heavily-booted SS men were stepping on him. It was a cruel sight but, at that moment, I only felt relief that it was not me. Drained of emotion and overwhelmed by the recent events, I did not feel any fear. I continued to follow the column for a short time longer, and then I turned back. For a moment I contemplated what to do next. The realization I was now alone began to sink in. A feeling of great sadness overwhelmed me, but the continuous danger of being caught on the street and shot urged me to move on, to survive.

In the late afternoon, the SS left the Jewish section of Tarnow. It seemed their task was, at least for the time being, finished. They had killed many Jewish men, women, and children, and deported those who remained to extermination camps. As I turned toward the *Judenrat* building on Folwarczna Street, I noticed the streets were deserted. I entered the wooden structure that housed the Jewish Council. People were milling around with bewildered expressions on their faces. Everyone seemed to be in a state of total shock. I ran into Vice President Lehrhaupt and told him my parents had been taken away to the railroad station. I asked him if anything could be done. He just looked at me and said nothing.

As evening approached, I left the building in a traumatized state. I made my way toward Urwana Street, toward the apartment I had left that morning with my parents. The day seemed to have been very long, so many things had happened, and now, bewildered, I crossed the little bridge on Bernandynska Street that led to Urwana 13. As I approached Urwana Street I saw the familiar railroad tracks and a train moving slowly around the bend. On each side of the boxcars I could make out the silhouette of an armed guard. My parents were in one of those boxcars, and I was watching the train carry them away. At that moment a sinking feeling overwhelmed me and I knew then I would never see my parents again.

Darkness fell on the city of Tarnow as I entered our apartment on Urwana Street for the last time. This was where I had lived with my parents for a year and a half. In a daze I looked through some drawers, finding my father's old Polish passport with the gold eagle on the front cover. Leafing through the pages, I saw the last entrance visa to Austria from July of 1938. I left the passport in the bedroom drawer, and wondered why we had not left this terrible place. I gathered a few possessions and placed them in a sack. On the way down I stopped to say goodbye to our Catholic neighbors, the Wozny family, with whom my parents had been friendly. I told Mr. Wozny my parents had been taken to the station and asked him if he knew where they were being taken. Mr. Wozny pulled out an old map of Poland and circled a town east of Rawa Ruska with a red pencil. The name of the town was Belzec. "That is the train's final destination," he told me.

I decided to go to my Aunt Sala's house on Lwowska Street in the center of the Jewish section. Sala was my mother's elder sister and she and Uncle Herman Handgriff had three daughters. The eldest, Rywa, left Poland before the war to settle in Palestine. The middle daughter, Hela, eloped in 1939 and escaped to the Russian section of Poland with her fiancé. There she had married and had a baby, but with the German invasion of Russia her husband was murdered in the town of Brzezany and so Hela returned to Tarnow with her infant daughter in December 1941. Now she shared the little apartment on Lwowska Street with her parents and lived in a state of great sadness and depression. I often heard her crying and singing sad lullabies to her baby. The youngest daughter, Renia, had finished high school and was looking for a job when the war broke out.

It was late in the evening when I arrived at my aunt's apartment. Not knowing who had survived, I was happy to see them alive. My aunt, uncle, and cousins, Hela and Renia, greeted me warmly. I told them my parents had been taken away and found out from them that my grandmother had been taken away too, as well as my Uncle Willek, his wife, and their two children.

Following the deportations, about eight thousand people had disappeared. Families were broken apart, and shock, confusion, and despair prevailed. All remaining Jews were ordered to move to the ghetto, located in the poorest section of Tarnow around Lwowska Street and which was now enclosed. A new fence surrounded the ghetto and two large gates, a guardhouse at each, were erected on the former bus square. Soon, new ID cards were issued and everyone was reassigned to work commandos. Again, I was assigned to a furriers' workshop, located outside the ghetto walls on Goldhamera Street, that became part of an artisan conglomerate called *Zentrale für Handelslieferungen* (ZFH). The ZFH was under the supervision of two German Komissars, Wagner and Milch. There were many workshops set up to provide items needed by the

German army, such as coats, uniforms, sweaters, and hats with fur linings. Every morning I left the ghetto with a column of workers assigned to the ZFH. We were counted at the gate as we left, and counted again in the evening as we returned. During the day, no one was permitted to leave the building where the workshops were located without a special permit. I was assigned to work in the fur-riers' section where fur-lined coats for the German army were sewn.

I worked twelve hours and around seven in the evening I returned to what had been my aunt's apartment in Lwowska Street and what was now part of the labor camp. The *Judenrat* had assigned an additional three people to this tiny and overcrowded apartment and so now I shared my little room with three other men who were strangers to me. My aunt, uncle, Renia, Hela, and her baby shared the second little room. My aunt tried to provide me with some food when I returned from work but food was rationed and bread was scarce and hard to obtain. The only way to supplement these rations was to sell the few personal items that I had taken with me from Urwana Street. I sold a coat and jacket through a middleman who risked his life to sell the goods to the Poles outside the walls of the camp. If caught, the penalty was usually immediate execution.

September 1942 approached, two months after the first deportations from Tarnow, and there was still no news about those who had been deported. I often thought about my parents, hoping perhaps they were alive somewhere. But I heard nothing about them and, slowly, I began to lose hope. Rumors about work camps in the East simply lacked credibility. There was no mail from anyone who had been transported and no one returned who could verify the existence of work camps. The transports disappeared into the night and there was only a stony silence from those deported. Rumors began to circulate among people in the ghetto about gas chambers and that something "terrible" had happened to the deportees.

On September 2, once again there were rumors of imminent deportations. On Tuesday morning everyone working in the ZFH had to turn in their ID cards. I was told that all ID cards would be returned in the evening. It was late in the evening when I returned to Lwowska Street. There was tension in the apartment. My uncle, aunt, and cousins had also had their ID cards collected and were now anxiously waiting to have them returned. Looking out of the window I could see uniformed SS men surrounding the Jewish ghetto. Late in the evening the *Ordnungdienst* began to return the ID cards. They stood in the courtyard in front of the crowded apartments and called out names. A late-night vigil did not produce my ID card. I realized I was doomed; without the card I stood no chance of survival. My uncle, aunt, and two cousins were also left without ID cards. They went to sleep, not knowing what the next day would bring.

I left the Lwowska Street apartment at about three in the morning. The eerie silence of the night and my sense of despair made me realize I had to do something if I wanted to avoid deportation. An inexplicable force guided me to the *Judenrat* building on Folwarczna 12. I crossed Szpitalna Street and approached the darkened two-story wooden building that housed the *Judenrat* of the labor camp*. It must have been four-thirty in the morning when I made my way up the stairs of the building. A streetlamp cast a weak streak of light that allowed me to see the stairway. Slowly, I walked up to the first floor. The place was empty, the rooms abandoned. After a while I began to descend slowly, not knowing what my next step would be. I knew of nowhere to hide and no one to turn to. I felt alone and terrified as I descended the stairs.

Suddenly, halfway down the stairs, in the light from the streetlamp, I saw hundreds of pink ID cards strewn about like trash on the stairs. In desperation I bent down and picked one out of the pile. I moved closer to the window. The ID card had a photograph on it

---

* In the summer of 1942, the Nazis renamed the Ghetto, Labor Camp.

and bore a round, green stamp with a Nazi eagle and swastika. The green stamp had blue pencil marks across it. I felt I had regained life. This was the stamp that made the difference between life and death. The invalidating blue pencil marks had to be removed. But how? I began to rub off the pencil marks, trying to erase them. When I finally left the building I could hear the sound of heavy boots on the cobblestone streets of the ghetto. In the distance I saw the SS battalions entering through the wooden gate and fanning out in various directions to collect the Jews.

Dawn came to Tarnow. The Jews were assembled on the former bus depot square. Men, women, and children whose ID cards lacked the Gestapo seal were sent to one side, while those whose cards bore the seal were sent to the other. We were ordered to kneel. This ordeal lasted till about five in the afternoon. The SS, Gestapo, and German green police took their time. The dogs barked and the screams of the SS were frequently interrupted by the sound of gunfire. By late afternoon those Jews without the Gestapo seal had been marched out of the ghetto. My turn finally came. I got in line and held my arm up high, displaying my ID card with the green Gestapo seal. The SS officer hardly glanced at it as I moved on to the temporary "freedom" of ghetto life. For now I was safe. I went to the apartment to look for my aunt, uncle, and cousins. It was empty; they were all gone. I never saw them again.

By September 1942 the ghetto was much reduced in size. The Jews of Tarnow were devastated. People appeared out of their hiding places to search for relatives or even a familiar face. Families had been decimated, mothers and children taken away, only the men were left behind. When I returned to my aunt's apartment I found eight strangers already occupying some of the rooms. I reclaimed my bed, and placed all my possessions under it. I was reassigned to the ZFH workshop on Goldhamera Street. As I marched out of the ghetto, Tekla stood on the street looking through the fence. Spotting me from a distance, she nodded and smiled at me.

In mid-September, people began to emerge from their hiding places in the Tarnow ghetto. I looked for my schoolmates Abras and Tulek. I went to the houses they had been staying in before the last deportation but they were occupied by strangers who knew nothing of my friends, not even their names. They had also disappeared. Sadly, I reflected that in the course of the last two months—from June 11 to the middle of September—every single person dear to me had disappeared. Out of my entire family, I was the only one left.

The September days grew shorter, with daylight ending at around seven. Upon returning to the ghetto, the dimly lit old houses cast a depressing mood, and the eight o'clock curfew added to the atmosphere of anxiety. I contemplated my options and listened to the rumors and stories about those who had tried to escape from the ghetto: some had been successful and had reached safety in Hungary, while others had been shot in the attempt. The *Judenrat* obtained new members to replace those who had been executed by the Gestapo. They issued new identification cards, and each inmate was assigned to a work place. The Gestapo was now numerous. They entered the ghetto in SS uniforms or civilian clothes, distinguished by their leather coats, shiny boots, and arrogant walk. They struck fear into the Jews and when word spread that Gestapo agents were entering the Jewish ghetto, the streets quickly emptied and the ghetto assumed the atmosphere of a ghost town.

As the days grew shorter and winter approached, I realized I was without winter clothing to protect me from the long, harsh months ahead. I sold my summer shirts and old shoes in order to buy a warm jacket, but my thoughts were on escaping the ghetto, something I could only hope to do with the aid of Tekla. A wall, a gate, and the police patrols now separated Tekla's world from mine. I lived in a "cage" while she dwelt on the "Aryan" side of occupied

Tarnow. As a Jew, my chances of escaping and surviving were very slim indeed. Nevertheless, one cold night in October a newly-found friend by the name of Fleischman, a boy of my own age who had dyed his hair blond, met me on the street to discuss plans for our escape from the ghetto. Despite the change of hair color, Fleischman's appearance made it difficult for him to pass himself off as a Catholic Pole. Nevertheless, he was optimistic of reaching the city of Lwow where he was unknown and where he hoped to blend in with the population. He was sure he would survive, and, a few days later, he disappeared from the ghetto and I never saw him again.

By early October, life in the ghetto (the ghetto has been renamed—Labor Camp) had resumed some semblance of routine. There was overcrowding, a lack of food, and new curfews. There were rumors about postcards arriving from recent deportees but no one had seen any such postcards. In late October I established contact with Tekla through a little window in the cellar of the ZFH building. Standing in front of the window, she could talk to me and I would not be visible from the street. She brought me food, bread, and occasionally some lemons I could sell in the ghetto. I was also helped inside the ghetto walls by our former neighbor, Mrs. Wahl, who, from time to time, prepared sandwiches for me. Her twin sons, Artek and Bronek, who had been my friends on Urwana Street, had survived the deportations and now the family had been relocated to an apartment off Lwowska Street.

In late October, new rumors began to circulate of an imminent action against the Jews of Tarnow. I decided to escape from the labor camp and asked Tekla to find a place for me. My decision was made in spite of the danger involved, as I had a feeling my chances of surviving the third deportation were slim. The date for my escape was set for the last week of October. Tekla provided me with her son's Polish ID card and his birth certificate; my new name was Bronek Nagorski.

The hour of my escape arrived; it was just after seven o'clock in the evening. Since the fences around the labor camp were guarded, I selected a sector that was in a dark area with fewer guards posted. As I approached the fence I saw Tekla's silhouette standing about three hundred meters away from the ghetto gate, looking nervously around, her head covered with her babushka. I approached the fence, climbed several feet up and jumped over. I immediately removed my Star of David armband and followed Tekla. It was close to curfew, the streets of the non-Jewish section of town were empty. Bronek Nagorski papers gave me a sense of security as we passed swiftly through the streets, Tekla walking ahead of me. When we finally reached our destination I entered a darkened corridor at the end of which there was a door on the left. We knocked softly and the door opened. A young Polish woman carrying an infant of perhaps eighteen months greeted me and showed me into one small room with two beds, two chairs, a wooden table and an outside toilet.

Several weeks passed and I remained confined to my room. Tekla came every day, bringing me food and the Nazi Polish propaganda newspaper, *Goniec Krakowski*. She pretended she was visiting her Polish friend. We conducted our conversation in whispers since any noise that might betray my presence to the neighbors. Proclamations posted on the streets of Tarnow warned the Polish population not to give shelter to Jews. Special units of police were on the look out for Jews and the danger of being discovered by a neighbor and possibly denounced to the Gestapo carried a death penalty for Tekla and myself.

Around November 14, Tekla came in excitedly telling me that the labor camp was surrounded by SS troops. She said she could hear gunfire, and no one was allowed to approach the labor camp's walls. Alone in the room, I felt safe for the moment, but the scenes of shooting and trains entered my mind. Several days later Tekla brought the news that the gates of the camp were guarded only by the German green police, with the Polish police and the Jewish *Ordnungsdienst* also manning the guardhouse. The action, the third in the last four months against the Jews of Tarnow, was over for the time being. I stayed with the Polish lady and her baby for another few weeks, but I was lonely and contemplated returning to the ghetto to share in the fate of the rest of the Jews of Tarnow.

Early in December, after six weeks in seclusion in one room, maintaining total silence during the day, I made up my mind to return to the Jewish quarters. I said goodbye to the kind Polish woman who had sheltered me for six weeks, and, with some clothes that Tekla had rescued from the Urwana Street apartment, I returned to the ZFH workshops on Goldhamera Street and reentered the ghetto which was now an *Arbeitslager,* or labor camp. The appointed labor camp commandant was SS Scharfführer Blache. *Arbeitslager Tarnow* was now divided into sections A and B. In one section lived the working group, in the other section the older people and women with children. The camp had about four or five thousand Jewish inhabitants—men, women, and children, although the children were not visible on the streets of the camp. Some of the smaller children had been smuggled out of the camp to be placed with Christian families. Others remained in hiding in the camp.

Once in the camp, I went to my aunt's apartment on Lwowska Street. There I met the new occupants, three men who shared my room and a family of four who occupied the other room. All were total strangers to me. I reclaimed my bed and hid my meager possessions beneath it—my stamp collection, which I kept under my pillow, my watch, and an old Austrian gold coin, which I always carried with me, tucked into the side of my shoe so it would not interfere with my walking.

My daily routine began at five in the morning. I lined up in the big square and then remained with my own designated work kommando. Each kommando was assigned guards to accompany it from the camp to the outside work sites. It was still dark as we marched out of the camp in rows of five. At the gate we were counted and I reached the designated building at ZFH within half an hour. The work began at eight a.m. and ended at seven p.m. when we marched back to the *Arbeitslager*. Upon reentering the *Arbeitslager* we were counted again and then returned to our living quarters. Washing facilities were minimal; there were no showers and the outhouses were often blocked up. Typhus and typhoid broke out in the camp. Large posters bearing the typhus sign appeared on apartments, warning people not to go in.

In December, winter descended on Tarnow and there was snow everywhere. The workshops continued to produce warm fur-lined coats and heavy woolen sweaters for the German armies fighting through the cold Russian winter. I presumed we were still alive because the Germans needed our skills for the moment. The German in charge of the entire workshop complex was an SS officer by the name of Koepke. The Jewish head of the workshop was Walter Reiss, who had been present at my Bar Mitzvah, and whose two brothers had already been killed in Tarnow. Reiss was able to communicate with the Nazi directors because he had been born in Berlin. He had been deported from Germany because his parents were Polish born. The workshops were frequently visited by Gestapo agents, one of whom, named Kastura, often came to the knitting department to order special items for himself and his family. Another agent from the Tarnow Gestapo branch was Grunow, a sadistic killer who sometimes accompanied Kastura on his visits to the ZFH building and shot at random in the Jewish ghetto. Whenever these Gestapo agents entered the building a warning would be passed around the workshops to be at your workstation and not be "loitering" anywhere else.

In mid-January 1943, I was assigned to work as a messenger

boy. I was given orders to notify the various departments of any impending requirements coming from the administrative office. I was at the disposal of the office and did not have to work in the furriers' shop. This job provided me with greater freedom of movement in the building and the ability to see who was coming to the building. My ability to move around the building also provided me with the opportunity to communicate with Tekla almost every day. At the designated time I would go down to the cellar which in the past had stored coal but was now empty. There were windows that reached street level. Tekla would linger on the side of the building next to the window, and I would talk to her. She could hear my voice but could not actually see me since I was below street level. She would leave food on the window ledge where I could reach it and she would also bring me the *Goniec Krakowski*. Trying to read between the lines, I would examine the newspaper carefully and orient myself to where the German armies were fighting. The Russian front was of great interest to all of us, since it was closest in proximity to Tarnow.

February 1943 started cold and gloomy in Tarnow. On the second day of February, I sneaked out of the ZFH building to purchase the *Krakauer Zeitung*. This foray into the forbidden territory of the "Aryan" section of Tarnow became a daily activity despite the risks it entailed. On this day, the newspaper carried banner headlines: *"Stalingrad Opfern, Finale."* The headline caught my immediate attention. I bought the newspaper and ran back into the ZFH building. There, in a secluded corner, I began to read the story. Up to this very point I had been totally unaware of the momentous battle for Stalingrad. It was with a sense of optimism that I read for the first time about German army losses and a major German defeat. The report offered a ray of hope in an ocean of despair. I shared the newspaper with the others in the workshop. But, with the harsh winter, the lack of food and warm clothes, the lack of any freedom, the loss of dear ones, and the slim chances of survival, this news gave me only a few minutes of uplift, soon to be crushed by the grim realities of my life.

Early in March a delegation of high-ranking German uniformed men and civilians inspected the ZFH workshops, asking questions about how many items were produced in each department. Anxiety and apprehension prevailed in the building. Rumors began to circulate as to the possibility that the ZFH would be closed. With the workshops closed, what would happen to us then?

There was an elderly man working in the office of the ZFH. His last name was Werner and he had come to Tarnow from Germany and spoke only German. It was rumored that he was married to a German Christian woman who lived in Germany with their son. One morning in May 1943, I noticed a handsome young man, perhaps seventeen or eighteen years old, coming in through the gate of the ZFH building. He did not wear a Jewish star and was well dressed. A few moments later Mr. Werner emerged from the office where he worked. The two embraced in the corridor of the ZFH, tears rolling down their cheeks. Later in the afternoon, I found out that his name was Horst Werner, the product of a mixed marriage, classified under the Nuremberg laws as a *Mischling*. The son had come from Germany to see his father for the last time. The sad reunion touched me deeply for the father did not live much longer.

August brought rumors that *Arbeitslager Tarnow* was to be liquidated. I awakened on September 3 and noticed the entire camp was surrounded by SS units. I could see them from the window, standing in full combat gear on Lwowska Street, guarding the camp so that no one slipped out. At seven in the morning, loudspeakers blared out that all Jews were to assemble in the old square, the same square from which all deportations took place. I was to join my ZFH work kommando and remain in the square. The sun rose late on this September morning as the last remaining Tarnow Jews gathered to meet their fate in Nazi-occupied Poland. Men, women, and children were herded into the square. As the SS units swept through the narrow streets, rooting people out of their hiding places, shots were heard, and more and more people filled the square.

In the early afternoon I noticed an SS man on a white horse who seemed to be directing the entire operation. Late in the afternoon, I was marched off with the others from ZFH toward the Tarnow railway station. As we marched through the narrow streets, people lined up on the sidewalk; the Polish Christian population witnessing the last Jews of Tarnow leaving forever. Suddenly, I caught sight of Tekla. She stood on the curb and our eyes met, perhaps for the last time. She had a helpless expression on her face. Soon I was herded into a cattle car, the door closed, and the train pulled out. For five hours we were packed tightly in the cattle car, with no idea where we were going. With no feeling of panic, I resigned myself to my fate. When the train stopped at the brightly-lit Krakow railway station, it was well into the night. We had arrived at Krakow-Plaszow concentration camp, a camp built on the site of a former Jewish cemetery. The Jews who had avoided being deported to Belzec were shipped here from the Krakow ghetto and the surrounding areas.

The eerie scene that followed can hardly be described. The SS guards that greeted us screamed orders, German shepherd dogs barking at their sides. We marched in rows of five up a steep flood-lit hill, and I suddenly saw a row of guard towers. Was this another planet—the Nazi New World? Before my eyes was a vast area surrounded by electrified barbed wire, with cement poles every few feet. Rotating searchlights added to the unearthly atmosphere. By entering this new planet of Nazi invention, I became what was known in the KZ culture as a *Katzetnik*—an inmate of a Nazi concentration camp.

Soon after arrival I was sent to a quarantine barracks. Stripped of all my possessions, including my wallet, a few photographs, my wristwatch, and my shoes, I lay down on the bare floor not knowing what to expect in the morning. The next morning, September 5, 1943, I was assigned a number that from now on became my new identity. My shoes were returned to me and, to my surprise, I found my gold coin still in its place. Later in the morning, released from the quarantine barracks, I was assigned sleeping quarters and a workplace, again to a furriers' workshop where coats and hats were made for the German army. The workplaces were located in a different part of the camp from the "residential" barracks. Neither site could be entered unless accompanied by a member of *Ordnungdienst*, who took their orders from the SS.

My sleeping quarters were in a large wooden barracks. The barracks were cold and dark with no effective heating system. The blanket was thin and hardly protected me from the bitter cold of a Polish winter. The mattress consisted of a sack filled with straw. There were three levels of cots placed vertically and extending in rows throughout the length of the barracks. Two people were assigned to each cot. My sleeping companion was Mr. Wahl, my former neighbor from Tarnow, who had been separated from his wife and sons, Artek and Bronek, who had been sent to Auschwitz.

My days in Krakow concentration camp began early. At five-thirty a.m. the block leader would shout for everyone to get up. Breakfast was black coffee accompanied by a small piece of black bread. This was followed by roll call on a large square directly adjacent to the barracks called the *Appelplatz*. Here the procedure of counting the inmates could take from thirty minutes to two hours. The accuracy of the count determined the length of stay on the *Appelplatz*. This became a very unpleasant experience as the cold winter months set in. Once roll call was over we were marched in rows of five to the work barracks where a work *Kapo* was assigned to supervise the work assignments, and a member of the

Ordnungsdienst stood by. The SS supervisor showed up anytime of the day or night and a Jewish worker that was idle could be executed on the spot.

Autumn was coming to an end and the harsh Polish winter beginning. The daily roll calls became a difficult chore as the cold wind penetrated every bone in my body. I waited, freezing and very hungry, for roll call to end. With only black coffee in the morning, watery soup at the half-hour lunch break, and a piece of bread given out now at night, I was tormented by hunger pains and began to think a lot about food. The days grew shorter and darkness fell early, enveloping the entire camp. The electric wire and the menacing towers remained visible from all parts of the camp. The only warm spot I could find was in the furriers' barracks so I felt fortunate to be assigned to an inside workplace. Sometimes I worked the night shift, from eight at night until eight in the morning. Our night work was often interrupted by a visit from Neuschel, the SS officer assigned to supervise us. He inspected the workshops, checking the production of each worker.

In late December the lights of the city of Krakow were readily visible from the camp's hilly location. My thoughts often wandered to the life beyond the barbed wire. The lights from the city brought back memories of a warm bed, real bedcovers, a little room with a stove, perhaps a table with some food, bread, butter, milk, and a little privacy. The lights seemed brighter than before. Perhaps the Christmas season had added a few more of them. Their distant glow provided me with a ray of hope, as well as envy. There was, after all, still some normal life beyond these barbed wires.

Early in January 1944, due to a short-circuit, the lights went out in our barracks. There would be no light in the barracks for some time. The evening soup was served by candlelight and we ate in semi-darkness. In the morning, I dressed in almost total darkness. It was very cold. Snow covered the camp and the ground was icy as we marched to the workplace. One evening we were not permitted to return to our barracks but were confined to our work barracks. An uneasy silence prevailed in the camp, interrupted from time to time by the sound of heavy boots. Deportations were taking place from other barracks and the silence of the night was punctuated by the screams of the SS guards and the voices of their Jewish victims. Then it all stopped. In our barracks a man started singing; somebody whispered in my ear that the singer's name was Bennet. He was a cabaret singer from Krakow. His soft voice pierced the silence, and in the darkness I recognized the melody, *O Sole Mio*. As it found its way that night into that terrible place, it brought back for a fleeting moment a fragment from a distant past of laughter with my friends and of my parents.

The next day, I learned the transports from KZ Plaszow had been sent to another camp, the Skarzysko Kamienne camp, which was attached to a large munitions factory, and that mostly women had been taken there. I also discovered that the SS man on the white horse I had noticed when *Arbeitslager Tarnow* had been liquidated was the Plaszow camp commandant, Amon Goeth. Goeth instilled terrible fear in all of us for he was known to pick up his hunting rifle and shoot the Jewish inmates at random from his horse. He made sure that inmates working outside the camp were thoroughly searched on their return. If food was found on any one of them, several would be executed.

In late January, I was given an assignment to bring water to our work barracks from the camp's well, which was situated close to the concentration camp's main entrance. The main food provisions and coal entered through this heavily guarded gate and I noticed some Poles coming into the camp with horse-drawn wooden carriages and wondered whether they smuggled food into the camp. Our route took us past the commandant's villa; a white structure perched on a little hill with a little veranda at the front. The villa's location provided Goeth with an extensive view of the concentration camp. Since I had to carry a big pot with another inmate, we placed two large sticks through the pot's handles and walked quickly so as not to be noticed by this sadistic man; Goeth often used his veranda to shoot inmates on sight.

Our barracks remained without light throughout February. It was bitterly cold. The man who had sung *O Sole Mio* had disappeared from my workplace, probably to the hospital. Others were also missing. Mr. Wahl received extra food rations, courtesy of his acquaintances among the *Ordnungsdient,* and he occasionally shared some of this food with me. We were subject to frequent night searches. The *Ordnungsdient* would enter the barracks and search wildly for any valuables that might have been smuggled in. I still had my watch, which I kept hidden in a pot filled with water. Afraid they would find it, I reached for it and gave it to a Jewish policeman. I was suddenly hit several times in the face and fell down.

In late February, I contacted a man named Balitzer whom I knew from Tarnow, where he dealt in gold and other black market goods. I handed him my only possession, the gold coin, and asked him if he could sell it for me so I could buy some bread in the camp. Three days later, I discovered that Mr. Balitzer had died. Now I was desperate; everything that I had of value was gone.

On March 20, during roll call, the work *Kapo* wrote down my work number. Not knowing what this meant, I was afraid I might be assigned to a *Strafkommando* (punishment work kommando). One could expect to last only a few weeks in the *Strafkommando*. My friend Frank from Tarnow had been assigned to one and, because of the hard work, was rapidly losing weight. But instead of the *Strafkommando*, I was assigned to a new work place on April 1, a barracks where broomsticks were made. The SS supervisor was called Mongol. He beat people at the workplace and was feared by everyone. There were two twelve-hour shifts, the work was very hard, and there was lots of dust in the air. A month later, my number was called out at roll call. I was to leave with some five hundred other men to an isolation barracks. Rumors circulated that we were going to be sent away, but where?

On May 3, I was ordered to attend roll call and was then marched off toward a railway station. I was ordered into a cattle car along with fifty others, divided into two groups of twenty-five. Each of us was given a loaf of bread and a pail was placed in the middle of the car in which we were to relieve ourselves. The journey into the unknown began. In the sealed boxcar I had no clue where I was, where I was going, or how much time was passing. The journey lasted perhaps three or four days, during which time we were we provided with a single bucket of water, hardly enough for fifty people. The thirst was horrendous. The train did not stop anyplace and the boxcar was filled to capacity. In these hot and crowded conditions, people passed out due to the bad air and the lack of water.

On the morning of May 6 or 7, the train finally stopped and the boxcars were opened. We were ordered to leave the car. I had great difficulty adjusting to the bright light of a sunny day but the shouting and blows of the SS guards allowed no time for contemplation. I had to move fast to avoid receiving strikes on my body. I caught a glimpse of a whitewashed railway station. The road leading from the station was deserted except for our column of five hundred Jews and SS guards with German shepherd dogs. A sign on the road caught my attention, it read; *Granitwerke Konzentrationlager Gross Rosen* (Granite Quarry Gross Rosen Concentration Camp). Clean little houses with flower boxes in the windows lined each side of the road. A glance through one of the windows revealed a table and chairs indicating that some form of normal life existed in this little German town. It seemed to me at that moment I was a million years away from my own life. I felt I was on a different planet or this was just a bad dream from which I would eventually awaken.

Surrounded by SS guards, I must have marched for an hour when I noticed the guard towers on the horizon. Soon, a concentration camp with barbed wire and a heavily guarded gate was in front of me. The gate opened and the sound of a Viennese march pierced the air, welcoming our column as we entered the gate. Clad in striped, pajama-like uniforms, emaciated figures were playing musical instruments. As I entered the new inferno my mind was set only on obtaining water. The column moved quickly through the gate into a roll call square surrounded by many SS guards with dogs. The SS greeted us with heavy blows and wild screams, the dogs by their side barking madly. This terrible ordeal lasted for several hours as the SS sadistically displayed their violent hatred for the new Jewish arrivals.

Close to sundown we were permitted to march toward the camp showers. Before entering the showers we were given a piece of stale bread. I grabbed the bread but, being so thirsty, quickly traded it for a sip of water. The shower attendant must have had experience with previous new arrivals who had traded their bread for a little water. A few steps led down into the showers. As I entered I experienced a moment of uncertainty, is this a gas chamber or a shower room? I glanced at the showerheads and I noticed droplets of water accumulated on them. Soon, cold water came gushing out and I opened my mouth in order to assuage my continuing thirst. Yells and beatings from the shower *Kapo* indicated that it was time to move on. I marched with the others into a barracks where, in a storeroom, I was given a set of bluish striped pajamas. Assigned to a bunk with another prisoner, sleep finally came. My tired aching body and shattered mind needed to rest, and perhaps to dream a dream of another world.

All too soon the shouts and blows of the block leader and his aid, another inmate, awakened us for roll call at four-thirty A.M. Thus on May 9, 1944, I experienced my first day on German soil, in a German concentration camp. But where was I? After black coffee and roll call, other inmates approached me. I began to ask questions: Where is this place? What kind of work is being done here? I soon learned that Gross Rosen was established in 1939 at a location between Breslau (Wroclaw) and Berlin. Most of the inmates were Polish and German nationals. There were no Jewish prisoners when I arrived. I was part of one of the first transports of Jews sent to Gross Rosen in many years to labor in the rock quarries. There was a crematorium at the camp; I could see the building with its chimney. I was told that they killed people by lethal injection. I also learned on the first day there was a *Strafkommando* where inmates were sent for minor infringements of KZ rules. The poor souls would usually last about two weeks, dying of hard work, beatings, and starvation.

It was difficult for me to adjust to life in this new concentration camp. The routine in the Gross Rosen camp, in the heart of Nazi Germany, was different from that of the Krakow-Plaszow camp. On the first day following the day of arrival, I was issued a striped camp uniform and my head was shaved. In the Krakow camp I had been spared this ordeal. In the Gross Rosen Camp, power was in the hands of the mostly German and Polish inmates who had already been there for some time. They were the food distribution block leaders, the *Kapos*. I became aware of the extent of anti-Jewish feelings among the non-Jewish camp population. This made life very difficult for the Jewish prisoners as the barracks leaders and their assistants punished us by reducing our rations, giving us the watery soup without the morsels of meat which came to the surface of the tureen only when it was given a stir. The overriding concern for me in Gross Rosen was to survive a day at a time, and then, through sleep, to escape for a few hours the reality of camp life.

About two weeks after my arrival at Gross Rosen I was again faced with a special roll call. The Jews from Krakow-Plaszow were assembled for yet another departure. Several members of our transport had died in Gross Rosen, so the count was now below five hundred. We marched out of the camp and were loaded onto trucks, destination unknown. Again I glimpsed the pretty houses. We passed by rolling hills and streams with rapid waters and, after several hours, arrived at a new camp. The sign proclaimed: Falkenberg Concentration Camp/Subcamp of Gross Rosen. I saw circular wooden structures but no traditional barracks. The SS camp commandant addressed us: We must build our own barracks if we wanted to sleep indoors. In the meantime we slept on hay in the circular wooden structures. My eyes searched for a chimney, the sign of a crematorium but did not find one. It was a ray of hope; perhaps there was a chance for survival.

The next day I discovered the other inmates of the camp were Greek Jews. They had been rounded up in Athens and Saloniki and sent to Auschwitz and then to this new camp. Some of the Greek Jews had been killed in Auschwitz; only the "fit" had been sent here to build roads. The rumor was that a tunnel was to be built in the mountains. On May 25, I was assigned to a road-building commando. I used a shovel to lay stones on the newly paved road. The stones were then crushed with heavy rollers, and thick asphalt was poured over them. The SS guards stood by as the German civilian foreman directed the actual work.

At the beginning of June, I was selected with others for a special work detail called the *Stollarbeiter,* or tunnel workers. I was assigned to the second shift—twelve noon to midnight. The work never stopped. At midday, I marched out with the others to my new work site. Walking up a rocky mountain, I saw one of my friends being carried by two men. He had been hit by a rock at the tunnel entrance.

The work in the tunnel progressed rapidly. I used an air hammer to break up large rocks left from the tunnel blasting and then loaded them onto a metal wagon. Two of my Greek fellow workers, Gerson and Nechama, were drillers whose task it was to drill long holes in the rocky soil. These were then filled with dynamite by the German civilian and blasted. This work was very hard. I was forced to enter the tunnel soon after the explosions when the air was very foul, full of dust and gasses from the dynamite. My eyes teared, and my lungs were filled with dust. Sometimes it was hard to breathe, but the SS guards and the German civilian foreman would force us to start work again. I loaded little carts that were driven away to a ravine where the rocks were dumped. The carts frequently tipped over and the rocks then had to be picked up with bare hands and taken out to the ravine.

Sometime in July, I move into a permanent barracks. I was assigned a bunk with another Jew from Poland. The other twenty-five people in the little room were Greek. I communicated with the Greek Jews in broken German but it was difficult to communicate well as some had picked up the concentration camp German jargon. When I returned from the night shift I often heard the Greeks singing mournful songs. I did not understand the words, but the melodies penetrated my soul and filled me with nostalgia and sadness.

In this forsaken place I struck up a friendship with a Hungarian Jew named Willy Woelner. Several transports of Hungarian Jews had arrived in the camp, many looking physically well. Rounded up around Budapest, they had been separated from their loved ones in Auschwitz. Willy lost both parents and his sister in Auschwitz but he had survived the selections and was sent to Gross Rosen to build tunnels. Willy and I were both sixteen and both alone. Assigned to the same shift, we used the air hammers to break up the large rocks, then loaded the smaller ones onto the wagons using shovels.

The tunnels were quite deep by now, with secondary tunnels branching out from the main one. Falling rocks presented a great danger because, once loosened by the blasting, they fell down from the roof of the tunnel hitting many of us. My shift included Gerson the Greek driller who could communicate with the Italian tunnel engineer, Mr. Ferrari, as they both spoke French. Ferrari, a man in his fifties, often screamed at us in his halting German. Then there was the German civilian worker who inserted the dynamite once the drillers had finished their work and also supervised the explosions. Most of the SS guards stayed at the entrance to the tunnel. They seemed much younger than those I had so far encountered. There was also a young German soldier working with us. He was perhaps nineteen, and he wore a German uniform without insignia. He walked with a cane and appeared to be recuperating from an injury. He acted as a guard for Willy and me and often escorted us back to the camp. There was an air of mystery about him. We often wondered why he was working in the tunnels with us, and looked for an expression of sympathy from him, but it never came. He always maintained his reserve, limiting himself to few words.

By September the weather was growing colder. I received a wonderful gift, a pair of shoes as promised by the camp *Kapo* to the tunnel workers. My feet were now better protected from the streams of water we encountered in the tunnels. My friendship with Willy grew. We talked about liberation and dreamed of a clean bed at night, of bread, butter, milk, and school. We shared the dreams of two boys who had just turned sixteen as we walked back to the camp from our night shift; two boys whose youth had passed them by and who were now hardened adults. As we left the tunnels at night we would gaze upwards at the stars and the clear sky and dream about being free. But we could not imagine how this could happen. Would the SS guards just disappear? Would freedom come at night with the camp commandant opening the gates and simply saying, "You are free?" I could not stretch my imagination to picture how freedom would arrive. It was all just a dream. But the moments of hope often clashed with somber thoughts. There were dark moments when I thought of how I would be killed. Would the penetrating bullet be painful?

In October, as the weather turned colder, my legs began to swell up and I had difficulty walking. I was afraid to report to the sick bay. I knew full well that inmates were picked up from the sick bay and sent to the gas chambers. But, after a few days, the swelling got worse, forcing me to report to the sick bay. Dr. Rubin, the inmate physician in charge of us, was from my hometown. He had treated my ear infections when I was little. He offered me a little soup, but when no further soup or any medicine came, I returned to work. I could not allow myself to be sick for the sick were not permitted to live long.

In late October there was a special roll call. We had to strip for the SS doctors who were going to select those who looked sick or weak and unable to work. I stood in line and the SS doctors examined me. Inadvertently, I made eye contact with one of them. There was that cold strange expression as our eyes met; the look of a wild animal observing its prey. I froze. What saved me on that occasion was the camp commandant's explanation that our group belonged to the tunnel commando. I suppose we must have been worth something in the Nazi's slave labor universe.

The ground froze as winter approached, and, in nothing but my striped pajamas and hat, I began to freeze during roll calls. The optimism and hope that Willy and I had shared during the summer months was gone as our chances of survival began to fade. When December arrived the ground was covered with snow. Totally isolated from the world outside the KZ camp, I had no way of obtaining news about the war. In late December work in the tunnels slowed down. Mr. Ferrari did not shout as much and the German dynamite expert also slowed down. I sensed a change coming. On January 1, 1945, my night shift did not depart for the tunnels. The camp commandant announced the entire camp had to be evacuated and would march off next morning. But where? After this announcement an air of uncertainty spread throughout my barracks. I wanted a change in my life but I was anxious about what would happen next.

The next day we lined up for roll call while it was still dark. It was an extremely cold winter. After the count we marched off in rows of five. The ground was covered with a blanket of snow and I had to march off without any warm clothes, wearing only the striped pajama uniform given to me at the Gross Rosen concentration camp. I walked briskly and the SS guards marched alongside to make sure that no one escaped. After a whole day our column arrived at another camp, KZ Friedland, another branch of the Gross Rosen camp complex. I received a bowl of soup and fell asleep on the wooden floor of a barracks. Early in the morning of January 3, we marched away from KZ Friedland. I caught glimpses of small towns and villages as we moved on. I tried to work out where we were by reading the signs: Waldenburg, forty kilometers east. I calculated that my column was heading south. As night fell we were forced into wooden sheds normally used to store farm equipment. There was standing room only and so I fell asleep leaning against the cold steel of a piece of farm equipment.

The following morning, I received a meager ration of bread. After roll call our group was separated and moved into other sheds. I was told to get some hay to put down on the floor. It was snowing outdoors, and we remained inside the cold wooden shed, our new "home." There was little time for reflection. Numbed by cold and hunger, I spent a whole week in this shed, somewhere between the city of Breslau and the former Czech border. By January 10, it was time to move on. Our column split into two groups with one marching off and the other staying put. We returned to the sheds. Willy left with the first group. I never saw him again.

On the morning of January 11, my group, surrounded by SS guards, moved on. I was part of a column in a group of five tired, wet and hungry prisoners. There was no time to think about the future. I lived just for the moment, not knowing what the next few minutes would bring. The weak, unable to walk, were shot and left on the road. For the first time in five years I saw German refugees fleeing west with their belongings. At one time Jewish refugees had been a familiar sight, but now it was the Germans fleeing the Russian armies. Seeing them with their horse-drawn carts brought back memories of Jewish families moving into the crowded quarters of the ghetto. The sight of fleeing Germans bolstered my hopes, perhaps now the nightmare would end with Germany losing the war! But was it all an illusion, a *fata morgana*? In my state of total exhaustion and hunger, in freezing weather, with the SS guards screaming and shooting, this could easily be an illusion. I fell asleep on a wet floor, to escape to a better world.

The next morning, after a few hours' march along a snowy road, we reached a small, clean town, where the houses had flower boxes on their windowsills. The well-dressed townspeople stared at us and I examined them in return. The sign at the railroad station said "Reichenberg." I was given a loaf of bread and a little marmalade and boarded another cattle car, one with a roof and open sides. I was overjoyed by the sight of the bread, having barely eaten anything in the past two days. The train did not stop until early the next morning at Turnov station. I recognized it as I had traded stamps with a collector from this town, which was in the former Czechoslovakia. The train remained at the station for many hours. We huddled together to keep warm in the bitter cold. The following day, the train stopped at another station, Pilsno. I knew where we were but I did not know where the train was going. As the train passed the station buildings someone tried to throw bread into our car. Somebody caught the bread and the train moved on.

On January 18, I stood most of the night watching the changing scenery, trying to judge the train's direction. The terrain became less flat with silhouettes of mountains visible in the distance. At one point we passed a large factory with tall chimneys spewing smoke. It was an isolated, flat area surrounded by a forest. There was no air raid damage here. In the morning, as the sun rose, the train came to a full stop. The doors opened and we were told to get out. The train had stopped at Mauthausen concentration camp. A few passengers in each boxcar had succumbed to the cold, from exhaustion, or from starvation and, so, emaciated figures in striped uniforms began unloading the dead from the train. Rumors circulated that almost half of the people on the train had perished. After several hours, we were told to get back into the boxcars. The SS guards positioned themselves on the train again. The train began to move, the sun was shining, and a cloudless blue sky was visible from the open boxcars. About half an hour into the journey we abruptly pulled into a railway station named St. Valentin.

When the train stopped, my eyes, always searching, looked up to see the blue sky above full of little specs. A large number of high-altitude planes were directly above the station. The SS guards jumped off the train and ran to the station's shelter. For me, it was an uplifting moment, I felt a new surge of energy, a ray of hope sparked by the sight of those planes flying above. For the first time in five years I witnessed planes bombing Nazi territory. The planes circled overhead, a sight that will stay with me forever. I would not have cared if the train were bombed. I had no sense of fear at that moment. Instead, a desire for revenge had emerged and I was willing to die as long as my SS tormentors were killed, too.

The air raid lasted about half an hour. The large round clock at St. Valentin station pointed to ten minutes to two, and then the train moved on. It was early in the evening when the train pulled into another station; the sign read "Ebensee." It was bitterly cold and snowing. A new group of SS guards took over and we were marched through the town of Ebensee, up the hill and into the new concentration camp: Konzentrationslager Ebensee/Subcamp of Mauthausen.

Ebensee concentration camp was surrounded by a forest. As I entered the camp I noticed a flat area where the roll call square (or, as it was called in the German camp language, the *Appelplatz*) was located. There were many barracks along the square. In the far corner my eye caught sight of a tall chimney and a crematorium. We assembled behind the crematorium and were then ordered to enter a neighboring wooden barracks in groups of five. Cold, hungry, and thirsty, I found myself in a large, chilly room with showers where cold water sprayed my freezing body. I was given a thin pajama-like uniform and allowed to enter block number 19. There was no glass in the barracks windows and a cold draft of air entered the barracks. Totally worn out, I placed my shoes under my bed and fell asleep on the wooden floor. I was awakened by loud screams and an order to line up. I immediately discovered that my most precious possession, my shoes, had been stolen. Desperate, I found a pair of wooden shoes and, slipping them on, made my way toward the latrine.

In the next few days I realized that I had arrived at Ebensee at the worst possible time. It was snowing outside and the mercury must have been below zero. From the *Appelplatz*, snow-capped mountains were visible but the picture-postcard scene struck me as ominous. Huddled in columns of five in the roll call square we were finally escorted through the guardhouse to the work site. My new workplace was a huge tunnel with many subdivisions and several railroad tracks running through it. I caught sight of large engines located in the side tunnels but had no idea what they were for. I was assigned to tunnel station number R6. My job on the first day in the tunnel was to clear the rocks from the areas that were still being excavated. After clearing the rocks I placed them in small wagons for another crew to take out of the tunnels. I discovered from other Jewish inmates that Ebensee concentration camp, as part of the Mauthausen camp, had been established in the summer of 1943 with the first Jews arriving one year later. I was told that there were approximately 2,000 Jewish inmates among the camp population of 16,000 and that the SS encouraged anti-semitism among the non-Jewish prisoners. There was a sickbay at the camp but it was not accessible to Jewish inmates, who were denied all medical care. The camp food was extremely bad with a watery, black liquid resembling coffee given to us before roll call, a watery soup served at midday in the tunnels and a wet, doughy bread with the same black liquid served at night after roll call. After twelve hours of grueling work, the constant hunger pains added to my physical exhaustion.

I found it impossible to bond with any of my fellow Jewish prisoners. If a temporary friendship did develop as a result of a rare flash of humanity, it soon ended, as the friend who walked beside you to work or shared your bunk suddenly disappeared. Death was the constant companion, particularly among the Jewish prisoners. In the first week of February a man in my column dropped dead as we marched along. The daily body count taken in the morning and in the evening, the cold, the hunger, and the long working day all took a terrible toll on the physical and psychological well-being of the camp inmates. At the roll call the most emaciated prisoners, "muselmen," in the camp jargon, were selected for death, taken away and killed, their bodies burned. I could see and smell the smoke from the crematoria at all times.

One evening in early March, as I returned from work, I was not allowed to enter my barracks for the night. An SS man stood in front of the door and told those of us assembled in the cold winter air that we were to be punished for leaving the barracks unclean. Because of this each of us was to be whipped before being allowed to enter our sleeping quarters. As my turn came I anxiously bent down and received five harsh lashes on my back with a horsewhip. In pain and tired from the day's work I soon fell asleep on my bunk bed.

On March 10, more transports arrived as inmates from other camps, some of them Jews, were transferred here. There were so many other nationalities. I worked with Yugoslavs and there were Italians in the tunnels, some of whom were civilian workers, others camp inmates. There were Poles, Spaniards, and Russians. This day I was transferred to Block 6, which meant I had to get used to another block leader, new *Kapos*, and other voices. They were all inmates and they used the same method of harassing their charges. The morning reveille always began with loud yells; "Get up! *Raus!*" ("Get out"). They used rubber hoses to make us move faster. Occasionally, I suffered these painful blows to my weak, emaciated body. On March 25, the entire block was punished. I did not know why. After roll call we were told to line up in front of the barracks. Each of us received five lashes with a leather whip on the buttocks, administered by an SS man. After this punishment we were allowed to reenter the barracks.

By late March, there was a hint of spring in the air. I caught a glimpse of some birds during roll call. The birds were freer than we were; they could simply fly over the fence and go their own ways. How I envied them! Completely isolated from the events of the war, I began to doubt I would survive. In April more transports arrived at the camp, and more people died every day. I wondered how it would all end. I could not picture liberation and what form it might take. I could not allow myself the luxury of illusion and I began to think more of death: would it come with a bullet or some other way? The entire camp was forced to witness the hanging of several inmates who had been recaptured after trying to escape. People tried to commit suicide by running to the electric fence, but were shot down by the guards before they reached the barbed wire.

Every night, we heard the air raid sirens. I saw no planes, but I was forced to go with the others to a designated barracks. We did not know whether this was a form of additional harassment or if a real air raid was taking place, but the loss of sleep took a terrible toll on me. On April 15, work crews left the camp to clean up the railroad tracks. When they returned, they told stories of bombed-out railroad stations. The Attnan Pucheim station, a key station on the route between Vienna and Salzburg, was hit several nights in succession. In the camp, cuts in rations led to an increase in deaths from starvation.

Another transport arrived on April 20. The new arrivals had long hair and wore civilian clothes and rumor had it that the new arrivals were engaged in some type of secret work. It was a strange sight because we all had our heads shaved and wore blue-striped uniforms. I received my monthly allowance of three cigarettes and immediately attempted to trade this precious commodity for a piece of bread, but was accosted by other inmates who brutally grabbed the cigarettes from me. Food rations were reduced once more; from now on there would be less bread and no soup. People began to eat grass or even the soft coal in the tunnels. The coal did not taste so bad and did fill me up, but it also gave me constipation. I felt less hungry after each ration of coal.

On April 28, as I stood on the square during roll call, three low-flying planes buzzed the campsite. There was no anti-aircraft fire from the SS guards. Perhaps liberation was close at hand. Had the camp finally been discovered? The next day, however, there was another public hanging. Once again, we were forced to march past the scaffold and turn our heads to look at the poor souls hanging there. The joke went round the camp that there was no escape except through the chimneys.

On Thursday, May 3, my night shift did not go to work. Something was happening; there were rumors of liberation. Very weak, I became quite panicky. My legs swelled up and I could hardly walk. I felt that in another few days I would be totally unable to walk. The following day, after morning roll call, we did not leave for work but were instead confined to the barracks. At six o'clock in the evening, a second roll call. Tension rose. I lay on my bunk with three other inmates. We talked little and I tried to preserve my energy. Saturday's roll call lasted three hours. Spring was in the air, but I felt very cold and lonely. I gazed off at the distant, still-snow-capped mountain, the Feuerkogel. The birds sang as we stood silently at attention. The SS camp commandant appeared and addressed us in German. The block wardens stood at attention and the entire camp fell silent, except for the voice of this SS officer. He warned us of an impending battle and urged us, for our own safety, to enter the tunnels. The rumor swiftly circulated that the tunnels were mined. The block wardens replied to the SS commandant that we, the inmates, would rather stay in the camp. For the first time in the history of this concentration camp, the commandant's orders were not followed. The SS guards surrounded the entire square. The guard towers were manned, the machine guns in place. At any moment, there could be an order to open fire on us. We would have had no chance of survival for we were defenseless, worn out human beings. But the machine guns remained silent, and the entire assembly was allowed to return to the barracks.

It was late afternoon when I got back to my bunk bed. My mind and my body were too weak to fully comprehend the enormity of the event. Could this be the prelude to freedom? I was unable to absorb the notion that I might soon be a free man again. I was only sixteen years old but had become an adult very quickly. The Nazis had entered my hometown when I was eleven and changed my life catastrophically. I lost my entire family and most, if not all, of my childhood friends. I witnessed man's brutality to his fellow man on a scale that no one, adult or child, should ever have to experience. As I lay on my bunk in the Nazi concentration camp at Ebensee, surrounded by nature's beauty, my mind and my body were too numb to absorb the reality of the moment. There was no joy for me that afternoon.

Sunday, May 6, 1945, was the day of my liberation: a day that will always live with me; a day forever etched in my memory. For the first time in almost three years I was neither awakened by the shouts of either the *Kapo* or the block leader, nor did my body receive any blows, and I did not have to take part in a roll call. It was a cool morning, although spring was in the air. The sky was blue and the camp was strangely quiet. The SS guards were gone from the observation towers, replaced by older looking men in *Wehrmacht* uniforms. I left Block No. 6 and made my way toward the main gate. I crossed the dreaded roll call square where a few people were milling around. The eerie silence of the square, normally punctuated by the SS screams, seemed unnatural. The camp was still surrounded by barbed wire.

I was unable to comprehend fully the enormity of this Sunday morning. My body was weakened and my mind unable to respond positively to the sudden change in the morning routine. I felt very weak as I approached the main gate, but I could still walk. People gathered around the gate. I was standing very close to it when an SS man motioned to me and three others to follow him. Too weak to resist, I left the main gate with three other inmates and entered a guardhouse located about fifty yards away from it. From this guardhouse the SS would observe the outgoing and incoming groups of prisoners and harass prisoners if they were walking too slowly, or if the row of five was uneven. Now deserted, I entered it to find a desk in the corner facing the large window overlooking the main road leading into the camp, a large, round clock on the wall, and all kinds of weapons—hand grenades, pistols, and rifles—scattered on the floor. The SS man ordered us to pick up the weapons and place them behind the guardhouse on the grass. I made several trips in and out of the guardhouse. Suddenly my eyes registered the unbelievable sight of a tank moving slowly up the road. Some distance behind it, I saw another tank. The first tank made a sharp right turn, to face the main gate of the concentration camp.

The gate opened and a figure in an olive brown uniform emerged from the tank. I glanced at the clock on the wall. It was eleven minutes past one. As hollow-cheeked figures emerged from the gate and swept the GI off his feet, I saw a large, white star on the tank and at that moment I became a free man.

CHAPTER 4

A Displaced Person in Italy
(1945 - 1949)

For the first time in six years I was free. Overwhelmed by the events transpiring around me, I stood in silence, watching the crowds of emaciated humans surrounding the American GI. They kissed his hands and touched his uniform as if touching a saint. Each of us wanted to make sure the man was real, the tank was real, and this was neither an illusion nor a dream created by our anxious minds. But my moment of reflection was interrupted by the sight of a crowd of newly liberated prisoners running in the direction of a large structure. They were headed towards the SS kitchen. When I entered the kitchen there were no guards in sight. There was hot coffee on the stove and some artificial honey cut into squares on the table, but no bread. The kitchen had probably been used that morning, since the coffee was still warm.

Soon, emaciated figures crowded into the kitchen, surged forward, and grabbed everything they could. I was able to put a small piece of artificial honey in my mouth. I also found some raw potatoes, which I quickly slipped into the pocket of my striped uniform. After about a half-hour I made my way back into the liberated concentration camp. In the meantime, someone had placed a large banner above the entrance to the camp, reading: "Long Live Liberty,

Long Live Austria." I also noticed elderly Austrians milling around the camp, World War One rifles over their shoulders. They must have come from the town of Ebensee. As I made my way back to my barracks, I saw GI's cordoning off the camp kitchen. They stood guard at the kitchen door, trying to prevent the starved inmates from storming it.

In the late afternoon, I lined up in front of the kitchen for my first meal as a free man. My turn came. In my old, worn out, metal bowl I found thick soup with large pieces of meat floating in it. The soup was rather fat and I ate it quickly, not being used to eating slowly. Soon afterwards I felt sick as my body had difficulty digesting the fatty and the large pieces of meat. That night I heard many former inmates moaning, vomiting, and complaining of stomach pains. Their first meal in so many years had not been such a great success.

On my second day of freedom I ventured out of the camp with another man. About half a mile from the camp I noticed a farmhouse and walked in and asked for some milk. In the kitchen were two SS men, still in uniform, who had apparently spent the night there on their way to a new life. Our eyes met, I looked at them, and we went our separate ways. I was too weak, too overwhelmed by recent events, and still too intimidated by the SS uniform to take any physical action against them.

The following day, I walked for about half an hour to the town of Ebensee. I wore only my wooden shoes and the dirty, striped pajama uniform but, as there were no mirrors in the camp, I was unaware of my disheveled appearance. The streets of Ebensee were full of American soldiers, some throwing around an odd-shaped ball, while others threw a smaller round ball and caught it in a large glove. Not having seen such a game before, I found it rather odd.

After spending a couple of hours in Ebensee I made my way back up the hill towards the camp. A stream of US army jeeps was headed in the same direction. Before I reached the top of the road, an American soldier motioned to me. I approached his vehicle. He was excitedly trying to tell me something in English. I could make out the words, "It's over! It's over!" but I did not know what they meant. It was May 8, 1945—VE Day. The Germans had capitulated, and the war in Europe was over. I finally grasped the meaning, but for me the war had been over two days earlier on Sunday, May 6. The next day, I witnessed the American Air Force celebrating the end of the war over the lake connecting Ebensee and Gmunden. American planes swept low over the lake in formations of three, only to soar high above the surrounding mountains and disappear beyond. Formation after formation performed this acrobatic act. I was very impressed to see these huge planes close up for the first time. As they flew away they seemed like silver birds; it was a majestic sight.

By May 10 the former concentration camp began to lose its residents. About two miles away there were cleaner barracks that had belonged to civilian employees. These barracks were in good shape and contained compartments that housed six people. As I entered the new barracks, I registered my name and was issued a certificate stating that I had been an inmate of Mauthausen-Ebensee concentration camp. I also had to state how long I had been imprisoned in other camps. Having completed this formality I became a bearer of a new ID card, that of a "former concentration camp inmate." Over the next few days the former non-Jewish inmates began to organize themselves by nationality: Poles moved together with other Poles, and Yugoslavs, Spaniards, and Italians formed their own groups for the purpose of returning home. Jews were deprived of their nationality.

Along with other Jews, I was content to wait and try to recover my strength and health. On the morning of May 13, I awoke with a high fever. My body ached and I had cold chills as I dragged myself

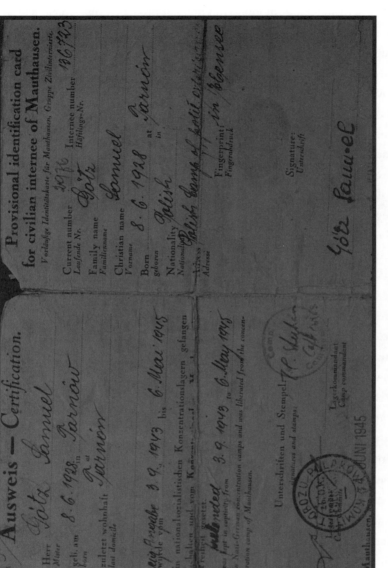

Certificate issued by American authorities following the liberation from Mauthausen/Ebensee concentration camp.

to a makeshift hospital room. There were few beds there, and people were waiting in a corridor. Former physician inmates, some of whom also looked emaciated, staffed this so-called hospital. After waiting for about fifteen minutes, I was taken into a little room where I was questioned about my health and my temperature was taken. I was told to wait. As I sat there, I learned that the very sick were being sent to hospitals in nearby towns. I soon noticed people being helped onto an open truck in front of the sick room. The doctors counted thirty sick people, and I was told that there was no space for me. Resigned, I waited, not knowing what would happen next. I felt very ill. As the truck began to pull out of the driveway I heard someone yelling; a man had just died. The truck stopped, a body was removed from it, and I was told to take the dead man's place.

It was about midday when the truck arrived at the nearby railway station at Bad Ischl. I saw a shiny train, with large Red Cross markings on the wagons. I boarded this former German army Red Cross train that had once transported wounded German soldiers. Inside the cars I saw bunk beds and was struck by how immaculate and shiny the train was. Helped by female nurses, I was given a clean set of blue-striped pajamas, which had previously been used by members of the *Wehrmacht*. The nurses acted in a professional manner, asking no questions of the former inmates but there was little interaction between us. Thus, one week after liberation, I found myself on a German hospital train, attended by German nurses.

I still had no shoes and one warm spring afternoon I left the train to stroll into the town. I gazed into store windows for the first time in many years and, in one of them, saw a pair of leather shoes. In my pajama striped uniform, newly liberated from a Nazi concentration camp, and with no money on me, I felt too intimidated to walk into a store and ask for the shoes from the storeowner. I returned to the train, still shoeless. After three days recovering on the train, a truck arrived and I was moved again. An hour later we arrived in a town called Bad Goisern where a converted girls' high school was to serve as a makeshift hospital. I was assigned to one of the small rooms, each of which contained six beds. Again, I was issued a new set of pajamas. The next day, along with others, I was taken to a municipal bathhouse. After a whole day of bathing, but no food, I was returned to the hospital.

The next day I underwent a physical examination. The doctor who examined me wore a German army uniform, with no insignia of rank. I weighed seventy-eight pounds. I received no medical treatment and the days in the hospital passed slowly. My diet consisted of oatmeal twice a day and some soup. There was no radio, no newspapers, and no news, so I decided to venture out of the building. Still without shoes, I strolled through Bad Goisern, a small Austrian town that had escaped the ravages of the war. The houses were adorned with pretty flower boxes in the windows, the streets were clean, and, as I crossed the town, I gazed upon green pastures and cattle. I stood and admired the tranquility of it all. On the way back to the hospital, children pointed at me and screamed: *"Da kommt ein katzettle!"* ("Here comes a concentration camp inmate!"). In my blue pajamas, barefoot, emaciated and without hair, I was a human aberration to the children in this little isolated town.

The next day I ventured out again. I decided to approach the farmhouses and ask for sugar and eggs. Some farmers were friendly, and I returned to my room to mix the eggs and sugar in a cup and enjoy a delightful cocktail. This success encouraged me to repeat the search for eggs and sugar. A farmer offered my companion, another former Jewish inmate, and me some pea soup, bread, and bacon. Soon after eating this I became violently ill.

On May 24, I was told that all patients would be returned to Ebensee. The next day, back in Ebensee, the truck dropped us off at the makeshift hospital and I caught sight of American doctors and

American soldiers. I was issued olive-colored fatigues and, finally, a pair of leather shoes with thick rubber soles. It had been six months since my shoes were stolen upon arrival in Ebensee. Soon after this, I found a place to stay in one of the apartments once used by the German civilian workers in the suburbs of Ebensee. Wearing my new shoes, and my new olive brown fatigues, I looked into a mirror and reclaimed my identity. I saw an emaciated face with very short hair. I hardly recognized myself—after all, I had not seen my face for almost three years. But for the last three years I had been used to seeing emaciated human beings, without hair, and reduced to the lowest human existence, so my appearance was not a shock. The KZ number was now replaced by my real name, Samek Goetz and I finally felt like a person again.

I began to contemplate my future. I was sixteen years old and alone. In the last six years my life had been transformed from that of a secure, middle-class, Jewish family, with parents, aunts, uncles, cousins, and friends, into a nightmare. From now on I had to make my own decisions; I was on my own in devastated post-war Europe. How would I make up for the lost years? My education had ended when I was eleven. My war experiences had not prepared me for regular adult life, despite the fact that, in a certain sense, my terrifying experiences had indeed abruptly transformed me from a child into an adult. How was I to view the world now? I had lost every human bond I had ever had and I had witnessed the total breakdown of man's humanity as I survived the Nazi concentration camps culture of cruelty.

There were rumors that trains were leaving from Salzburg for Italy and that from Italy you could go on to Palestine or even America. I recalled that my father had two brothers living somewhere in America although I did not know where. So, barely three weeks after liberation, I decided to leave Ebensee for Salzburg and perhaps Italy, and then America, in search of my uncles.

My journey to Salzburg took a long time even though Salzburg is only about one hour away from Ebensee. I made my way to the town of Voeklebruck, located on the main railroad line between Linz and Salzburg, but the Austrian railroads were in total disarray. The tracks were damaged and priority was given to freight trains transporting essential goods. Thus it took several hours to get from Ebensee to Voeklebruck, where, along with a few others, I received ration cards for bread. After several more hours a freight train arrived. It finally left the station at six in the evening, and took all night to reach its final destination, Salzburg. Salzburg was undamaged except for the bridges over the Zalzach River. A stranger to the city, I followed a group of former inmates who knew of an office that would provide us with information and possibly food and clothing. After searching for a while we arrived at a small apartment that served as a makeshift distribution center. I was given a sweater and instructed to proceed to Kaiser Joseph Kaserne, the collection point for transports to Italy. I entered an old, red brick structure with a dark and cold interior. I registered at the desk as a displaced person wanting to go to Italy. I was a stateless person and no one asked me why I wanted to go to Italy. The barracks were depressing, and I was anxious to leave as soon as possible.

Within a week of my arrival I was told that the train for Italy would be leaving the next day. I arrived at the station early in the morning. The train I boarded was probably of pre-World War I vintage, its old boxcars drawn by a steam locomotive. There were quite a few Italians returning home and about one hundred Jewish refugees. I did not know any of them; some had been liberated in Ebensee, others in Mauthausen. When I asked where they were going, the answer was, "to Palestine." My supplies on the train consisted of a small amount of sugar, a dozen eggs, and some bread. The train stopped for a few hours at Innsbruck, and then continued toward the Brenner Pass where the Italian border guards waved it through. Once on

Italian soil, the returning Italian POWs began getting off at various points. I celebrated my seventeenth birthday on June 8, 1945, as a displaced person in Italy.

When the train arrived at Bolzano, the one hundred Jewish displaced persons were told to disembark. At the station we were picked up by a truck bearing a US insignia. Before long we arrived at some clean barracks which also housed black GIs. This was our overnight stop. In the morning, the trucks returned and we were off again. Late in the afternoon, we arrived in Verona. After spending the night there we moved on to Modena where I spent my first night on the floor of a Jewish synagogue. In the temple, someone gave me a Jewish Star of David, which until a few months before had been a stigma but now it gave me a new sense of joy. It was the next day in Bologna when I first noticed soldiers with a Star of David patch on their shoulders. I learned that these were Jewish soldiers from Palestine, attached to the British army.

At Bologna, I was registered and received a displaced person's ID card issued by the Allied military government. I was housed in a tent camp supervised by the United Nations Relief Rehabilitation Administration (UNRRA). This organization became my temporary surrogate family. UNRRA was supposed to feed us, house us, and provide us with the means to return to normal life. Thus, I began life anew in Italy. Little did I know it would be another four years before I shed my newly acquired identity as a displaced person.

It was sometime in the middle of June that I arrived in Rome from Bologna. From the station I was taken to a place called *Cinecitta*, a temporary transit camp for displaced persons. Many years later I learned that *Cinecitta* was where many fine Italian movies had been made. But on this day in June 1945, the movie set was occupied by a throng of homeless people. I spent my first night on a cement floor in a large building. I was given an army blanket with the letters UNRRA stamped on it. I also received five hundred lira and a small package from Delasem, an Italian-Jewish relief organization. I was excited to be in Rome, but soon after my arrival rumors spread that those of us from Austria would be leaving soon, destination unknown. I was sorry to hear this news, as I wanted to see Rome, having read so much about the city. I still had vivid recollections of the book *Quo Vadis* in which the author described life in Rome under Emperor Nero, the struggles of the Christians, and the spectacles in the Coliseum.

Again I boarded a train. Soon, with an UNRRA official on board, it began its journey south. I observed the names of the Italian towns and the train stopped for several hours at Bari but I did not dare leave the station. Late in the evening we finally arrived at the dusty railway station of Nardo. Trucks bearing the UNRRA insignia picked us up at the station. After about half an hour we stopped in front of a two-story brick building. There were several people in the building, apparently expecting us. I was registered again, given some underwear and a straw mattress, and assigned to a room. With some difficulty I found my new lodgings in an upstairs loft, a tiny, hot room, in a small, whitewashed stucco house. I had arrived at Displaced Persons Camp No. 34, in the fishing village of Santa Maria di Bagni, in southern Italy, at the very heel of the Italian boot. Two weeks after leaving Austria, I began my new life and took up a new residence I would occupy for the next four years.

When I awoke the next morning, a lizard was playing hide-and-seek above my bed. My white-painted room was very small and contained no furniture. The toilet facilities were outside. Even early in the morning, I was struck by the oppressive heat. I decided to leave the room and made my way down a narrow cobblestone street to the center of the village. On my way there, I found the road blocked by a herd of goats. When I finally reached the center of the village, I caught sight of the ocean, its surface reflecting the sunlight like a vast mirror. With the sun basking in the blue waters, the incoming waves foamed as they struck the rocky slopes of the shoreline. It was a sight of great natural beauty: the blue sky above, the ocean stretching out beyond the horizon. I was unaccustomed to such sights, and experienced an unusual sense of euphoria as I admired the spectacular view. My daydream ended as I recognized the little building where I had arrived the previous night and received my mattress. Small stucco buildings were arranged in a horseshoe-like figure around the village square. I saw no stores, but a water pump stood out proudly, a little off-center. Goats were tied up to a pole next to some houses.

I received my ration card at the UNRRA building, and was told where to find the kitchen. I was issued a pair of yellow undershorts, some sort of army fatigues and a pair of socks. I decided my ill-fitting, yellow underwear would have to serve as swimming trunks, and so, barefoot and skinny, with my hair rapidly growing back, I made my way down through the rocks to the inviting waters of the Ionian Sea. Once wet, my undershorts became quite transparent and revealing, but this did not bother me for now. This was the first time I had ever bathed in an ocean, and over the next few days as I began to get sunburned, the immediate past seemed to fade away. The excitement of the water, the sun, and the warm air temporarily replaced the cold, dark misery of the barracks.

In the course of the next few days I began to get to know a little about the village and the surrounding area. Santa Maria was a small and impoverished fishing village. The fishermen left early in the morning and returned late in the evening with their catch. Unfortunately, there was hardly any market for the fish. The DPs had no money and the wealthy Italians who had visited here before the war no longer came. The coastline was for the most part low and sandy. Olives, grapes, figs, and almonds grew in the region although, in late June 1945, fishing appeared to be the main activi-

N. 0142   MOD. B

Soggiorno degl Stranieri in Italia

Séjour des Entrangers en Italie – Foreigners' sojourn Italy Aufenthaltserklärung für Ausländer in Italien.
(Circolare Ministero Interno. 13/49066 del 19 gennaio 1947)

Provincia di _Lecce_
Province - Province - Provinz

Comune di _Nardò_
Commune - Municipality - Gemeinde

Cognome _Gotz_
Nom - Name - Zuname

nome _Samuele_
prénom - surname - Vorname

paternità _Josef_
paternité - paternity - Vater

maternità _Gutfind Eugenia_
maternité - maternity - Mutter

nato a _Tarnov (Polonia)_
né (née) à - place of birth - geboren in

il _8-6-1928_
le - date of birth - am.

di nazionalità _polacca_
de nationalité - nationality - staatsangehörigkeit

di condizione _celibe_
de condition - condition - zivilstand

luogo di provenienza _campo concentramento Mathausen_
lieu de provenance - coming-from? - herkunftsort

data di ingresso in Italia _4 agosto 1945_
d'entrée en Italie - date of entrance in Italy - Einreisedatum in Italien

scopo del soggiorno _profugo_
but du séjour - reasons of sojourn - Zweck d. aufenthalter

luogo di dimora in Italia _S. Maria al Bagno (Nardò)_
lieu et censure in Italie - place of dwelling in Italy - aufenthaltsort in Italien

con i congiunti di età non superiore ai 16 anni, a tergo indicati, che accompagnano il dichiarante.
avec i enfants, indiqué au verso, d'age non superieur à 16 ans, c accompagnent le déclarant.
with children, whose age does not surpass 16 years of age, listed on the back of this form as living with the declarant.
mit auf der rückseite angeführten, nicht über 16 jahre alten angehörigen, die den erklärer begleiten.

La presente ricevuta deve essere esibita ad ogni richiesta degli organi di Polizia.
La présent reçu doit être exhibé sur toute demande des organes de la Police.

Il possesso di essa costituisce la sola prova della dichiarazione di soggiorno.
La possession de ce reçu constitue la seule preuve de la déclaration de séjour.
The possession of said receipt is the only proof of the present declaration.
Der Besitz desselben, nur, den Beweis der anmeldung.

Nardò , il _19 febbraio_ 19.7

Il Commissario di P. S.
(Dott. ...)

Firma e qualifica dell'Autorità di P. S.
Signature et qualification de l'Autorité de Sûreté Publique
Signature and qualification of the Police Authority
Unterschrift der Polizeibehörde

ANNOTAZIONI

Non ... ordinate annonarie
carte annonarie

AVVERTENZA — Il titolare è vivamente pregato di rendere il presente documento, all'atto dell'uscita dall'Italia, consegnandolo al funzionario addetto alla verifica dei passaporti alla frontiera. Tale restituzione è richiesta unicamente a scopo statistico.
AVERTISSEMENT — Le titulaire est vivement prié, au moment de quitter l'Italie, de consigner le présent document au fonctionnaire qui verifie les passeports à la frontière. Cette restitution est uniquement demandée dans un but de statistique.
NOTICE — The possessor is requested to return this document to the passport official at the frontier, on leaving Italy. Such restitution ...

Sam's permit to stay in Italy as a displaced person.
Issued on August 7, 1945.

Sam (on right) in a
displaced person camp,
seven months after
liberation from
concentration camp.
December, 1945.

Sam's roomates in the
displaced persons camp in
Santa Maria. From left: Sam,
George Aleksandrowicz,
Oscar Haer, Ludek
Goldstein, and sitting,
Nathan Kohn. Picture taken
in December, 1945.

Sam is employed as a
nurse aide in a well-baby
clinic—Italy, 1946.

Sam and Gerti (his
future wife) in Santa
Maria D.P camp. Sam
is 18 here and
Gerti is 15.

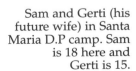

UNRRA REFUGEE
HOSPITAL
ST.MARIA DI BAGNI.

2nd.February.1947.

To whom it may concern.

This is to certify that Mr. Goetz Samuel has been employed in the a/m hospital as nurse-aid since December 1945.

During this period of time he has shown to be a very keen worker and of a great help while assisting the nurses and the doctors in treating the patients. During this time he has aquired a good experiance especially in M.I.Room treatments where he was working.

Any person wishing to employ him in his capacity may be sure that Mr. Goetz Samuel will not fail to satisfy his employer.

Dr. M.Rosenzweig

666
Medical Officer in charge
of the M.I.Room

U. N. R. R. A.
Accommodation Center
Santa Maria di Bagni,(I.T.34)

Dr. M. Bondi

Senior Medical Officer

B. Kenny

Camp Nurse Supervisor.

Certificate of employment in D.P. camp, Santa Maria, Italy
(Sam's first job in Italy)

3o September 1947

To Whom It May Concern,

This is to certify that Mr.GOTZ Samuel,born 8.6.1928 in Poland has been working in Palese M.I.Room from 1oth March 1947 until t-day in capacity of Nurse-aide and interpreter.
During his work in M.I.Room he has shown much interest in his work, has been very dilligent,skilfull,intellegent and honest.
He seaks.and writes fluently Polish,German,English and Italian, and have very good knowledge,heoretic and practical,as a Nurse-aide.
We should warmly recommend him for this kind of job.

/Dr.Na... Arnold/

Sam's certificate of employment as nurse aide at D.P. camp.
Palese, Italy, 1947.

ty. I found a small store off the village square that had dried fish for sale, but no bread. Nevertheless, the villagers seemed content.

I gradually began to adapt to my new routine. Every day I ventured barefoot to the ocean, lay in the sun, and allowed my hair to be bleached straw blond. Every day brought new displaced persons to our little fishing village. We all watched as the new arrivals descended from the trucks. I did not expect to recognize any familiar faces, but some people did. They would find a lost friend or relative and embrace tearfully.

One morning in late July I was sitting on the beach when I spotted a girl in a green bathing suit. She had light brown hair and a pretty face. I approached her and we began a conversation in German. She told me she had been born in Vienna but had lived in Italy for the last six years. I told her I had been born in Poland, had been liberated in Austria, and had come to Italy in late June. With these few words, my friendship began with Gerti. Her family had survived the war in Italy by hiding and had been fairly treated by the Italians, even to the extent that an Italian Fascist official had saved them from being deported to Auschwitz. Her mother now worked in the UNRRA office and her father helped out in the kitchen. We began to see each other quite often, usually meeting at the beach.

The search for relatives and families was an important part of the daily activities in the DP Camp. Lists of survivors located in other camps were posted on the wall next to the UNRRA offices. People tried to locate distant relatives in America, and the receipt of a letter from one of them would add to the day's excitement. In the middle of August I decided to return to Rome. There were rumors of relief packages there for those who had arrived from the newly liberated concentration camps. I promised to return for Gerti's fourteenth birthday on September 7.

Along with three other new friends, I boarded the six A.M.

train for Rome at the dusty little station in Nardo. The train stopped frequently and took two-and-a-half days to reach Rome. Tired and dirty, I took advantage of the public bathing facilities at the station to clean up. The following day, my friends and I registered with the UNRRA office. It was another three days before I received my UNRRA package, which I promptly sold. Invigorated by the thought that I had become temporarily "wealthy," I began searching in store windows for a fourteenth-birthday gift for Gerti. Finally, a pretty little automatic pencil, green in color, caught my attention. I walked into the store and purchased it. It was the first time in five years I had walked into a store as a free man without fear. Proud of my accomplishment, I decided to return to Santa Maria in time for Gerti's birthday.

Again the train made frequent stops but finally, after three days, it arrived at its final destination, Lecce. I was told that since this was Saturday night there would be no connecting train to Nardo until Monday morning. Disappointed, I decided to walk the thirty-five kilometers and was joined by others who did not want to spend the night at the dusty railroad station. After walking all night, I finally arrived in Santa Maria at the break of dawn. Tired, with swollen feet, I approached the freestanding water pump in order to splash some water on my aching body. A few minutes later I saw Gerti.

In October I began to work in a medical inspection room. My job was to assist the nurses in their treatment of the many sick patients. I prepared bandages, brought the implements to the rooms, and cleaned up the tables following the treatment. I soon learned how to dress a wound, clean up a sore and put on bandages. I also assisted with the disinfection of newly arrived DPs. I would spray their clothing with a DDT gun and stamp their ID cards "FFI" (free from infection). I made friends with several boys my age living near me. We all talked about emigration—but where to? Palestine? America? The gates were closed, and no one wanted to return to Poland, or even stay in Europe.

As 1945 drew to an end, more displaced persons arrived in our camp. There was a vibrancy in the life of the DPs. It consisted of a mixture of hope, the desire to begin a new life and, at the same time, the realization of the terrible losses we had all sustained during the years of the Nazi regime. Stories began to emerge of how people had survived the war. Accounts of heroic partisan activities in northeast Poland, the hardship in the forests, and the struggle to obtain food, weapons, and shelter emerged. Fights among the DPs occasionally punctuated our bittersweet lives when someone recognized a former *Kapo* and sought retribution. But we were all too close to the actual events to be able to assimilate the enormity of our own experiences.

Surrounded by the beauties of nature, abundant sunshine, and the desire for new life, romances sprang up and weddings performed in the crowded rooms brought back memories of lives and families back home. By early 1946 babies started being born at the hospital located in a nearby DP camp at Santa Maria di Leuca, manned by refugee physicians with some Americans acting in an advisory capacity. The new mothers would be instructed by the English, Canadian, or Italian nurses how best to care for the infant. Since I spoke English, I was assigned to the well-baby clinic so I could help to translate the instructions to the new mothers.

A makeshift post office opened next to the official UNRRA building. People would line up eagerly, hoping for a letter from an American relative. A blue airmail stamp on an envelope would create a stir since it signified a letter from America. I discovered my brother, Bernard, was alive in Poland. He had survived in Russia, joined the Polish army, and was now living in Poland. I also began to correspond with Tekla, who had saved my life during the war. Even though she could not write, a letter from her would arrive every week, telling me who had survived in Tarnow and who had come back. She wrote about the new Jewish committee in Tarnow that helped returning Jews to find each other.

One day I received a letter from America. Excitedly, I read the letter from my Uncle Emil, my father's older brother who had left for America at the turn of the century. He had found out where I was from the list of DP camp inmates which was compiled and circulated in the United States by JOINT, an organization based in the US which provided aid to the DPs. He wrote in German and asked what my plans for the future were, offering to help me if he could. I was very excited. I had come to Italy with the hope of finding my father's family in America and now it had happened. I replied to my uncle in English (my English lessons as a child in Poland began to pay off). More eager than ever to improve my English, I read books such as *Immortal Wife*, the story of John C. Fremont and began to pick up conversational English from the English and Canadian nurses with whom I worked.

In June 1946 the US consulate in Naples opened for business. I promptly sent in my immigration application and three weeks later I received number 1540 on the Polish quota. This indicated a waiting period of at least five years since very few visas were allocated to the Polish quota. Soon after the consulate opened, my friend George Aleksandrowicz received his immigration visa. George's father had arrived in the US in 1940 and so George received a preferential visa. I said goodbye to him with great envy, but I was glad he was finally able to get out of post-war Europe.

In the summer of 1946 I moved into a small room in the building where the medical inspection facility was located. I shared the room with a friend, Natek Kohn, who had survived the ghetto in Lodz and later, Auschwitz, and had been liberated finally in Ebensee. In September 1946 I received a letter from the American consulate in Naples informing me I had been classified as a minor orphan. This entitled me to preference within the Polish quota.

New refugee transports arrived almost weekly. The new arrivals told of their return to Poland after liberation and the pain of not finding anyone, as well as that of not being well received by their former neighbors. Most of the new arrivals were anxious to get to Palestine as quickly as possible. Kibbutzim began to form in the DP camps. Most were divided according to their brand of Zionist ideology: left, right, or center. All the members had one goal in mind: to get to Palestine and resume a normal life. A United Nations Commission visited the Santa Maria DP Camp in order to find out how many Jewish refugees wanted to go to Palestine. I was contacted by my first cousin, Rywa Handgriff Loew, the only survivor of my aunt's family, who had lived in Palestine since 1934. Rywa began to write letters to me and immediately sent me a package of clothes.

We began to take our beautiful surroundings—the ocean, the beaches, the sun, and the clear skies—for granted. The euphoria of the first few months after liberation was replaced by the realization that no lost relatives would be found, and uncertainty about the future now began to have a depressing effect on all of us. Illegal escapes to Palestine from the nearby Italian ports began full scale. Many of the kibbutzim lost half of their members overnight. It was a hush-hush operation, but it was well known to most of us.

Early in the morning an UNRRA truck took several Jewish refugee children, including Gerti, to the high school in the nearby town of Nardo and returned them to the camp around three in the afternoon. I worked in the medical inspection room, or ambulatorium as we referred to it, as well as the well-baby clinic, which took place twice a week in the same room. My job was to take patients to the university clinic in Bari. I made these daily trips in an ambulance and helped to translate the patients' symptoms into Italian, all the while anxiously awaiting letters from America.

Early in March 1947 we were advised that DP Camp Number 34 would be liquidated and that we were to be transferred to Camp Palese, near Bari. After a three-hour ride on UNRRA trucks, we arrived at a new location. The many barracks lacked toilet facilities and the roofs were made of tin. It appeared they had served as temporary quarters for army units during the war. My only consolation was the camp's vicinity to the town of Bari, an important Italian port on the Adriatic coast. Liberated in 1943, the town had resumed normal life, stores were full of merchandise, the opera house was open, and the movie theaters were showing the latest American films. In July 1947 US visas were issued to those classified as minor orphans, but only those who were nearing the age of twenty-one. Since I had only just turned nineteen, I was not granted a visa.

In September, the displaced persons camp in Palese closed. The remaining DPs were transferred to the nearby town of Barletta. This community of about 75,000 was very close to the ocean although the camp, a former Italian army barracks, was located farther inland. The large rooms were divided by small plywood partitions. Families with small children and married couples had very little privacy and conversations passed easily through the thin walls. I shared my little room with my friend, Natek, and another friend, Ludek, who had also been liberated in Ebensee and who had traveled with me to Italy. We shared the same hopes of speedy resettlement and resumption of normal life. Gerti and her parents were billeted just across the hallway from me.

In November 1947 I was offered a position as a secretary for the Organization and Rehabilitation through Training (ORT) schools. My job consisted of typing schedules for the classes, maintaining lists of attendance, and finding space for the new schools that were being formed. The desire to learn a trade and possibly use it in America, Palestine, or Canada, ensured the schools a large attendance. Meanwhile, many people were leaving for Palestine. Their

Sam employed as secretary of ORT schools.
Picture taken in 1948.

Sam (seated in front row, third from right) attending a
course in agrictulture in preparation for emigration to
the USA. Picture taken in 1948.

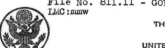

In reply refer to:
File No. 811.11 - GOETZ, Samuel
LMC:mmw

THE FOREIGN SERVICE
OF THE
UNITED STATES OF AMERICA

AMERICAN CONSULATE GENERAL
Naples, Italy, February 24, 1948.

Mr. Samuel Goetz,
   Campo Profughi No. 3,
      Barletta (Bari).

Sir:

    I have received your letter of January 4, 1948 to
the President of the United States concerning your immigration visa case. Your letter has been referred by the
White House to the Department of State and thence to this
Consulate General for attention and reply.

    The records of this office show that you registered
at this Consulate General on May 24, 1946 on the Polish
quota waiting list and have been identified as a minor
orphan and a displaced person. The documents that you
have presented have been examined and approved.

    Due to the smallness of the Polish quota and the
large number of persons who registered at this and other
American consular offices ahead of you who are also charge-
able against the annual quota provided by law for Poland,
it is not possible to predict when your turn to apply for
a visa may be reached. When your turn is reached and a
quota number is available for issuance of a visa to you,
you will be called to apply for a visa.

                Very truly yours,
          For the Consul General:

                H. W. Carlson,
                American Consul.

Reply to a letter Sam sent to President Harry Truman on January 4, 1948.

ORT

Organizzazione Rieducazione Tecnica

UFFICIO SUD ITALIA
SOUTHERN ITALY OFFICES

BARI __July 28th '49__

CORSO VITT. EMANUELE, 49
TELEFONO 11331
TELEGRAMMI ORT IT - BARI
CASELLA POSTALE 344

TO : WHOM IT MAY CONCERN
FROM : O.R.T. SOUTHERN ITALY, BARLETTA
SUBJECT: <u>TESTIMONIAL</u>

   , This is to certify that Mr. Samek Goetz has been employed by this Organisation since January 1948, as secretary, for the Barletta Camp schools.

   Mr. Goetz has always proved himself to be an honest and willing worker, devoting long hours to his work.

   My trust in him, during the time of his employment has always been complete.

   His work has been highly appreciated, both by our Headquarters and by myself.

   He is leaving the employment in order to e-migrate to the U.S.A. and I do not hesitate in recom-mending him, for any future employment.

J. ERLICH

Certificate of employment for Sam who worked at ORT in Italy.

INTERNATIONAL REFUGEE ORGANIZATION
DISPLACED PERSONS CENTRE
BARLETTA

28th July 1949

CERTIFICATE OF EMPLOYEMENT
=========================

TO WHOM IT MAY CONCERN

      Mr. GOETZ Samuele has been employed in this Camp as Secretary to O.R.T. from 27th January 1949 to 28th July 1949. His work has allways been excellent.
      He has been willing, honest, cheerful and has shown tact and patience to a degree seldom found in a man of his years.
      He was a tremendous help to me when we were organizing and building the schools, which now deal very efficiently with approx 300 students and in addition has helped me in dealing with many matters not concerned with his employment.
      In my six years work with refugees if I were asked to name the best one I have known I would say without hesitation, in every respect, Mr. Samuele Goetz.
      He is now departing for the embarkation centre from where I whish him a speedy departure.
      Should he ever need any letter of recommendation etc. or nay additional detail of his work or general conduct he can use my name as I also know many other officials with whom he has worked who are of the same opinion as myself, some of them are from the U.S.A. and can be contacted personally.
      I take this oportunity of thanking him on behalf of the organization and whish him the best of luck in his new country.

HT BEECH/mmb

H.T. Beech Capt.
Camp Director CAMP DIRECTOR
BARLETTA CAMP

Certificate of employment and farewell letter from
Displaced Person Camp Director H.T. Beech, Capt.

departure was kept secret and, although reports would soon arrive of their capture and detention by the British on the island of Cyprus, people continued to leave.

As 1947 drew to a close, living conditions in the Barletta camp deteriorated. The lack of privacy in the barracks, the meager food rations, and the lack of emigration opportunities had a depressing effect. A little more than two years after the end of the war and liberation from concentration camps had not provided the DPs with the opportunity to resume normal life. Children were being born in DP camps, marriages were taking place, yet no emigration possibilities had emerged, except for illegal departure for Palestine with the prospect of detention on Cyprus. Then, in November, the UN vote to partition Palestine provided a measure of hope. The news from Palestine, of the call for an armed struggle to prevent the establishment of the Jewish State, caused excitement and anxiety among the Barletta DPs.

Congress was debating the admission of 100,000 DPs to the United States. I purchased the *Rome Daily American* to keep abreast of the debate. The provisions of the bill called for admission preference to be given to agricultural workers. This provision prevented many Jewish DPs from entering the US and so the ORT schools began to offer courses in agriculture. Tractors were brought into the Barletta camp so that students could learn how to operate the various types of agricultural equipment. I enrolled in the course and learned how to drive a tractor and, upon passing the final exam, I received an ORT diploma as an agricultural worker.

At the beginning of 1948 Gerti and her mother received notification from the American consulate in Naples to appear for a pre-immigration physical examination. They were to be granted visas on a Czech quota since Gerti's mother was born in Czechoslovakia and Gerti qualified as a minor child. My own emigration status depended on the fate of the DP Bill in Congress. My status as a minor orphan within the Polish quota had apparently lost its validity, so I was resigned to wait. I continued to work for ORT and when the director of the schools, Mr. Ehrlich, left for Palestine, I assumed his duties. At the age of nineteen, I became an acting director of the Barletta ORT schools.

I began to think about my future. I had not attended school since my underground education in Tarnow. My formal education had ended in 1939, when I completed the fifth grade. So now, almost three years after liberation, I began to think seriously about my future. My American family asked in their letters what I intended to do once I arrived in America. One day on a visit to the town of Barletta with Gerti, I noticed an advertisement in a window for lessons in English Literature by an Italian professor. I signed up to begin lessons. My Italian professor, a friendly, middle-aged Italian man, perhaps in his forties, had a diploma from the University of Naples that read *"Dottore in Lettere."* With his Italian-accented English he taught me Chaucer's *Canterbury Tales* and we spent much time on Shakespeare. I discovered a new world of knowledge which fascinated me and added to my eagerness to learn. Twice a week I went to Barletta to meet the professor in the single room he rented from an Italian family and the two hours I spent in that room flew by. This was the beginning of a long quest to make up for all the years I had lost.

Sometime in September 1948, I left for Rome. I was given the opportunity to spend two weeks in a sort of sanatorium where children were given good food, medical care, and were exposed for a few weeks to the luxuries of a better life. I arrived in Rome and was taken to a villa on the outskirts of the city. The villa, located on Via Cortina di Ampezzo, had beautiful gardens and housed children from DP camps in its many rooms. For the next two weeks I was fed sumptuous breakfasts, lunches, and dinners. I began to explore the sights of Rome such as the Roman Forum and the Capitol. It was exhilarating just to be in a city where life pulsated at a normal tempo. The contrast of my life in the Barletta DP camp and the two weeks in Rome provided me with a glimpse of a normal city life — illuminated boulevards, movie houses, restaurants, and little cafes where the Italians chatted, relaxed, and perhaps met a date. I watched the city come alive in the early morning, the stores lifting their metal shutters, the bakeries displaying their freshly baked goods, the streetcars and buses carrying people to work. It was a view of normal life that I only vaguely remembered from before the war. Nine years had passed since September 1939 and I now dis-covered exciting aspects of life I had never before experienced. I shared my experiences of Rome with Gerti, telling her about the Via Nazionale, where I saw Italian boys and girls courting each other on a *passegiata*, the wide boulevards, the coffee houses, and all the other sights I had seen.

News of the newly passed Displaced Persons Act in the US Congress created excitement in the camp. There were many ques-tions about the formal requirements for emigration. At the same time, the constant news about the war in the newly established state of Israel created tension and anxiety. There was an informal drive to recruit young volunteers out of the DP camps, and I contributed part of my ORT salary to the Israel Defense Fund. News from rela-tives in Israel was anxiously awaited while word of new arrivals who had died in the War of Independence was greeted with great sadness.

In March 1949, Gerti and her mother were granted US immigra-tion visas. Gerti would sail for America at the end of April. After four years of waiting there was finally some hope of leaving the DP camps. The doors to Palestine, now Israel, were finally opened; Canada and Australia, too, began to admit some of the former refugees. My roommates, Natek and Ludek, left for Australia. Natek, who had lost most of his relatives during the war, was tearfully reunited with his brother in Melbourne. I shared my little partitioned room with another boy, Abram Mendelson, who had come to the DP camp from Romania. At the end of March I received a registration number under the new DP Act. The news arrived via JOINT. I was also asked to provide documents showing I had not been indicted for any crimes in Italy. My uncle provided the required assurance of housing and employment in the US. These formalities were necessary in order to obtain an immigration visa.

In April, Gerti and her mother received their US immigration visas. As the Austrian immigration quota was low, Gerti's father had to wait his turn to enter the United States, which meant the possibility of several more years in a DP camp. Gerti, her parents and I boarded the train in Barletta for Naples. Gerti's father was quiet on the train, deep in his thoughts, not knowing when he would see his wife and daughter again. After changing trains in Foggia, there was little joy as we approached Naples six hours later. Although I was excited that Gerti was able to leave Europe for America, I was sad about our separation, although I was confident we would see each other again very soon.

On our last day in Italy together, Gerti and I decided to go to Pompei. We hired a horse-drawn carriage and took in the sights. It was a bittersweet afternoon for us. It was four years since we had met on the beach in Santa Maria and now we were going to be separated as we met the challenges of a new life. The next day she boarded the SS *Sobieski,* the old ship that would take her to America. I caught the train back to Barletta with Gerti's father. We passed the train ride mostly in silence, both of us with our own thoughts. I returned to the Barletta DP camp depressed, facing a void in my life. I had shared the last four years in Italy with Gerti, we had spent every day together, meeting after she came home from school and I returned from work. Now all I could do was to look forward to receiving her mail, and I waited daily for the mail call.

In June I turned twenty-one and was summoned to appear before a commission in Rome that processed displaced persons. In Rome I registered at the International Refugee Organization office (IRO) and was given an appointment for the next day. At the appointment I was asked questions such as: "Have you ever been a member of the Nazi party?" and, "Have you ever been a member of the Communist party?" To which I answered, "Of course not!" I took a physical examination, which included X-rays to check for TB, a blood test for syphilis, and a mental competency exam given by a psychiatrist. Afterward I returned to Barletta.

In her first letter from America, Gerti said very little about America and her new life. Our correspondence continued in Italian and, although my Italian grammar was barely adequate, I managed to express how much I missed her and how I was longing to be reunited. In July, I was notified through the US JOINT office I had been granted my US immigration visa. Four years after my liberation from a Nazi concentration camp, and after four years in Italian displaced persons' camps, I was finally going to leave the European continent. By August 15 I was once again on German soil, this time at Camp Grohn, Bremerhaven, having arrived by train the previous night. Camp Grohn had the flavor of America. I felt very special surrounded by the Stars and Stripes flags which were hoisted at the camp entrance. There was an air of optimism, hope, and new beginnings, mixed with the question: "What now? What will I do in America?"

The buses from Camp Grohn left early in the morning of August 29 for Bremerhaven. I boarded the *General CC Ballou*, a Liberty-class ship, along with several hundred DPs from Germany and the rest of those who had come from Italy. After almost two weeks on the Atlantic Ocean sea-sickness had afflicted many, but in the late hours of Saturday afternoon the *General CC Ballou* entered New York harbor. The awe-inspiring view of the Manhattan skyline and the sight of the cars along the Long Island highway produced a mixed feeling of exhilaration and nervous expectation. Despite the misery of seasickness, my excitement as the boat approached the American shore could hardly be contained. After so many years my dream was finally coming true! On Sunday, September 11, I rose early. Immigration officials arrived on the boat at eight a.m. Each of us had to show an embarkation card before being allowed to enter the "land of the free," and take the first step into an uncertain future. I stayed below with the officials to help with translations so I missed the Statue of Liberty. As the boat approached the entrance to the harbor I experienced a feeling of exhilaration but also of anxiety about my future and my new life in America—about the relatives I had never met and about seeing Gerti who was now on the West Coast. Finally, cleared by the immigration officers, I left the boat for American soil and a new world of uncertainties.

Part Two

America

CHAPTER 5

A New Life in America
(1949 - 1969)

September 11, 1949 was my first day in America. It was a beautiful Sunday morning. After a rough ten-day voyage across the Atlantic, I stepped off the Liberty ship *General CC Ballou* and onto the firm soil of America. I was greeted by a group of relatives whose faces I was seeing for the first time. From the photographs sent to me at the DP camp in Italy I found myself matching the faces with the names. I immediately recognized my Uncle Emil, who corresponded with me. He was my father's eldest brother who left for the United States when my father was four years old. There were several of my cousins, including Milton and Betty Goetz. Milton, the son of Uncle Emil, was rather tall and handsome and impressed me with his warm smile and strong embrace. Betty, in her mid-thirties, kissed me warmly as if she had found a long-lost brother. I was also greeted fondly by my cousin Rose Goetz, who was one year older than I and the daughter of my Uncle Sam, my father's other brother who was not at the pier. As I embraced my Uncle Emil, I felt a warm sensation permeating my whole body, my eyes were moist, and a bittersweet feeling came over me. These relations were the extension of my mother and father and I had yearned for the embrace of my family for so many years.

I soon found myself sitting in a car with my newly found family on our way to my uncle's house. I was too overwhelmed to appreciate the sight of the Manhattan skyscrapers. The two-story stucco house, located at 2846 Harrington Avenue in the Bronx, became my home for the next four months. Upon arrival I met some additional family members, including my uncle's wife Hattie who struck me as being very frail. The conversation that day avoided questions about our European family or my wartime experiences, focussing instead on lighter subjects such as the World Series. It was interrupted by a long-distance call from Gerti in California. She wanted to know all the details about my arrival and my family. We had so often talked about this moment in Italy that she wanted to hear my impressions of my dream as it came true.

I slept late the next morning. The sun was bright when I awoke and I found myself alone with my Aunt Hattie, my uncle having gone to work. I was greeted with a glass of pineapple juice (a novelty for me) and some toast. I decided to explore the neighborhood and soon learned that the house was located about five minutes walk from the Westchester Square subway station. On the way there I spotted a market in front of which flew an American flag. As I looked at the flag a sense of pride and satisfaction overwhelmed me. I was finally in America, and I did not even have to carry an identification card! I was a free person with a name but no documents. This was a strange feeling for someone who had just come from a place where identification cards could determine the right to live or die.

I soon found a job as a salesman at Saks on Thirty-fourth Street in the men's furnishings department. At night I took the bus to Fordham Street where Theodore Roosevelt High School was located and where I had enrolled in classes in American literature, English language, and math. The classes had many foreign-born students, mostly older than I. I enjoyed the classes but the presentation of the material and the methods of testing were new to me. I was anxious to learn, however, and the excitement of being in America and going to school provided me with enough positive energy and motivation to overcome any difficulties.

The snow began to fall in New York. In early November my Aunt Hattie, died leaving my Uncle Emil inconsolable. The two of us then shared the two-story house—my uncle, whose life had come full circle, and I, who was beginning to meet the challenges of a new life in America. Sadness prevailed in the house. His two sons, Milton and Norbert, often came to the house to comfort him. How could I, who had lost all my loved ones a few years ago, console my uncle? My own feelings were frozen. Somehow, during the war, surrounded by constant cruelty, I had learned to suppress my emotions in order to survive.

In January 1950, I decided to join Gerti in California. The trip to Los Angeles began at a Greyhound bus station in New York City. It was snowing, gloomy, and cold. I boarded the bus early in the morning which was to take the southern route to California. New to America, I watched with interest as the bus rolled through the little towns. The first stop introduced me to a little café with a soda fountain. A long counter with tall barstools faced the fountains where ice cream, drinks and whipped cream were dispensed. Across the room, in the corner, a jukebox dispensed music unfamiliar to me and so different from the tunes I had heard in Italy.

As the evening approached and darkness descended, I adjusted my seat for the night's sleep. Light drizzle left a mist on the bus windows, yet I was able to notice a change in the scenery as we entered the southern states. My eyes caught a sign on a water fountain: "For Whites Only." When the bus came to the next stop I noticed another similar sign as I entered the station's restroom. I was confused by these signs proclaiming "Whites Only" and "Colored Only" but I did not dare ask the other passengers about them. As the bus moved on, I reflected on my time in Bolzano, Italy, in June, 1945. Four weeks after my liberation from a Nazi concentration camp, I had spent my first night on Italian soil with black American GI's. Now, on American soil, the separation of the races left me perplexed. My American Dream, the proud feeling of seeing the Stars and Stripes in Camp Grohn and, later on, fluttering in the wind in front of an American market in the Bronx, was incongruent with these signs.

The bus traveled through Oklahoma's vast flat land punctuated with oil derricks. On the third day, New Mexico's horizon revealed a mountain chain and clear blue skies. As the bus stopped in Phoenix, I stepped out into a warm breeze and noticed with relief that the restrooms lacked the sign "For Whites Only." Four hours later I arrived at the Los Angeles Greyhound station where I was met by Gerti's Aunt Hilda. Hilda, in her late forties, had arrived in the United States from Vienna in 1940. She embraced me and then took me to her one-story white stucco house, where she prepared a little room for me. Later that afternoon Gerti arrived from work and, after six months of separation, we were reunited.

Since Gerti had arrived in Los Angeles in May 1949 she had been enrolled in classes at Los Angeles City College. Her mother was ill and her father still lingered in a DP camp in Italy, awaiting an American visa, which would come in 1951. In the meantime, Gerti had to work as well as continue her education. I also enrolled at LACC and set about trying to find a job. My first semester at LACC ended in the middle of June just when the news of the North Korean invasion of South Korea broke.

Gerti and I were married on July 25, 1950 in a civil ceremony at the Los Angeles Municipal Court. The next month, on August 11, we had a religious ceremony that was performed by Rabbi Sonderling of the Fairfax Avenue congregation, a kind man who offered to hold the ceremony in his own home so that we, penniless immigrants, would not have any expenses. Soon after the ceremony, Aunt Hilda provided a reception and invited many of her friends to celebrate with us. Now married, I left Aunt Hilda's home and Gerti and I shared the apartment with Gerti's mother. We found jobs in downtown Los Angeles. I worked in a May Company stock room while Gerti sewed shirts in a factory.

Early in September I was notified by the local draft board I must attend an army physical examination on Santee Street in downtown Los Angeles. The examination was quick. A psychiatrist asked me about any problems and I told him briefly about my three years in a Nazi concentration camp. He seemed unimpressed. The rest of the physical went fine, except for some remarks by the army doctor that I was underweight. In the end though, as a full-time student I was granted a college exception. In 1952, Gerti transferred to UCLA and I followed soon afterwards.

On Sunday, October 26, 1953, as I sat in a maternity waiting room in the Cedars of Lebanon hospital in Los Angeles, I reflected on my first four years in America. A nurse announcing that Gerti had given birth to a son interrupted my thoughts. A few minutes later I got a glimpse of an eight-pound baby boy with a scratched nose. It was exactly ten past two in the morning and I had to make a class at UCLA at eight a.m. With great excitement I returned to my apartment off St. Andrew's Street to share the news with Gerti's mother. So that our son would bear the name of his ancestors, we named him Joseph Samuel; Joseph after my father who perished at the age of forty-three in a Belzec gas chamber and Samuel after my uncle.

Although ill, Gertie's mother took care of our son while we worked and went to school. Gerti graduated from UCLA when Joey was three months old. I continued with my studies. The subjects were hard and I had difficulty in finding sufficient time to study. I worked thirty-two hours a week and carried sixteen units every semester. My classmates were GIs, many of them veterans of the European theater of war. Noticing my accented English, they asked me where I had been during the war. But I was not yet ready to discuss my war experiences, and my answers were brief.

In January 1955, I graduated from UCLA's School of Public Health. The commencement ceremonies took place in June, and thus, ten years almost to the day after my liberation, I received my Bachelor of Science diploma. It had been a long, hard road. Gerti and I, who had been fortunate to survive the Nazi destruction of Europe's Jewish children, were both now graduates of the University of California. In June 1955 our finances were meager; we had a few hundred dollars and one child. The future, however, looked bright. The memory of the recent past seemed to fade, at least temporarily. My newly acquired US citizenship and college graduation propelled me, at least superficially, into the American way of life.

Yet, I continued to receive letters from Tekla, reminding me of my recent past. She told me who had returned to Tarnow, and who had not returned. I yearned to know if any of my classmates or ghetto companions had survived the war. But the news was bad. They had all disappeared, deported to Nazi extermination camps, and now they lived only in my memory. I often repeated their names so as not to forget: Abras Koch, Tulek Siedliskier, Moniek Rinder, Edek Dar, and the girls: Sianka Kleinhandler, Lilli Maschler, Lilli Schweber. I often wondered if I was the only human being in the world who remembered them? They were so young, given no chance to enjoy the fruits of life. I tried to search for my friends from Urwana Street, Artek and Bronek, with Tekla's help, but in vain. There were rumors circulating in Tarnow that Artek jumped the train taking him to Auschwitz but he never returned to Tarnow in search of his parents. He most likely perished. I was very sad not to be able to find these two friends of mine.

In June 1960, wearing cap and gown, I stood in a University of Southern California auditorium to receive my Doctor of Optometry degree. Gerti, her parents, and our son, Joey, who was now almost seven years old, accompanied me. On that beautiful day in Southern California I reflected on my not so distant past. So much had happened in my thirty-one years of life. Eighteen years earlier, across the ocean on another sunny day, the sky had darkened. My thoughts were interrupted as my name was called. Eighteen years ago, when my name had been called, I had been given a blue rubber stamp with a Nazi swastika on it—a temporary reprieve from death. This time I was handed a diploma.

My daughter was born in January 1961. We named her Eugenia Helen, after my mother who had perished in a Nazi camp along with my father. I wondered what I would tell our children about their paternal grandparents when they grew up. Should the heavy burden of memory be handed down to them? In the Jewish tradition we pass down the teachings of our ancestors to the next generation; but recent history carried too great a weight! However, life must go on, and I hoped that the memories would fade with the passage of time.

In 1962 I joined an organization, The 1939 Club, consisting mostly of Jewish survivors from Poland. The organization's activities were directed toward the raising of funds for those orphans who had miraculously survived the war and reached Israel. Most of the members of the organization were older than I and had a better understanding of Jewish life before the World War II. Conversations frequently turned to prewar life and our wartime experiences. For the past ten years, while a student, I had seldom related my own experiences to anyone. Except for the GIs, my fellow students were too far removed from the harsh realities of the war.

Since my arrival in America, I had immersed myself in the task of bringing up my family. Joe was now nine years old and Genie one year old. Gerti was working as a librarian and I had begun to practice my profession as an eye doctor. Then news came from Israel about the capture of Adolf Eichmann, a man responsible for the death of many Jewish men, women, and children. It was seventeen years since the end of the war but suddenly this news and the accounting of the Eichmann trial, including details of how many children died, triggered an emotional response in me and my memories returned with a fury. The television pictures showed a man who betrayed no regrets, no feelings, as he viewed film footage of the liberated concentration camps. The past was beginning to interfere with the present as I thought back to June 1942, when I became destined to be one of Eichmann's victims. As busy as I was with my daily life, the strong impressions of the past persisted in returning. I begin to think about the preservation of that memory, perhaps a collection of documents and books about the Nazis and the Jews. I proposed the establishment of a fund at UCLA for the purpose of collecting and preserving such documents at the UCLA library.

In October 1966, my son reached his thirteenth birthday and the time for his Bar Mitzvah. He recited his Haftora at a small synagogue, Mogen David, in West Los Angeles. A reception followed; it was a festive occasion. For a moment my mind turned back to my own Bar Mitzvah, twenty-five years previously. Then, there had been no music and few smiling faces, but we persevered with Jewish tradition. I had presented my Haftora (the weekly prophetic reading) in that small room before a congregation who knew that, if discovered, their punishment would be death. But for the moment we remained defiant and, at least on that day of June 1941, victorious.

In 1969, twenty years after Gerti and I left Europe, we decided to return to show our children where we had lived and where Gerti and I had met. Joe was now sixteen and Genie was eight and we felt we were emotionally ready to go back for a visit. In fact, I was quite excited to show Gerti and the children Ebensee where I regained my life and my freedom. There was no trace of the camp but the mountains above the camp revealed the tunnels, now closed to visitors. Ebensee, now in Austria, is surrounded by a mountain range whose main peak, Feuerkogel, towers majestically above the valley. It was Feuerkogel that I saw every morning from the *Appelplatz*. At the time it had had an ominous appearance, now it was simply magnificent. We went on a cruise of the lake. The young Austrian guide explained the history of the Salzkammergut region without mentioning a word about the former concentration camp where thousands had died. My son gestured to me: "Why don't you tell them, Dad?" I decided to remain silent.

We traveled around Europe. The English Channel and the beaches of Dunkirk made an impression on me, as did the beaches of Normandy. I showed the children Rome where I had first arrived in June 1945 and where twenty years earlier I had received my American visa. The visit to Italy had a special meaning for Gerti and me. For me, Italy represented the post-Holocaust period and a period of healing. I arrived in Italy about a month after liberation and the sun and ocean replaced the smell of camp life and the ruins and gloom of post-war Germany with its concentration camps still smoldering. It was also, of course, where Gerti and I had met and fallen in love.

CHAPTER 6

An Assault on Memory

In the early seventies our son Joe attended UCLA and often brought home the college newspaper, the *Daily Bruin*, which I had also read as a student. One day my attention was caught by a written debate among the students regarding the Holocaust. Several publications and books had recently been published, questioning the historical facts about the Holocaust. Some of these writers questioned the existence of gas chambers in the Nazi extermination camps; others denied the loss of six million Jewish lives, and still others simply called the whole thing a "Holocaust hoax." The distortions and denials were extremely disturbing to me and caused me to reflect on my own experiences and the loss of seventeen members of my family in June 1942. Did my classmates and family just evaporate into thin air? I began to immerse myself in the subject, trying to understand the motivation of the writers. Could it be that an organized effort was being made to distort recent history, even while the victims, as well as the perpetrators, were still alive?

I began to reflect on my own experiences. My formative years, from the age of eleven through sixteen, had been spent in Nazi-occupied Europe. I had watched Nazi troops enter my hometown, and I had witnessed the SS guards escape from the

UCLA ALUMNI AND
DEVELOPMENT CENTER
405 Hilgard Avenue Los Angeles California 90024 213/825-3901

April 20, 1977

Dr. Samuel Goetz
9200 West Pico
Los Angeles, California 90035

Dear Dr. Goetz:

Thank you so much for requesting information on our Endowed
Chair Program at UCLA.

Enclosed is some information which will give you an overview
of our chair program. Please contact me when you need more
information.

Within the next two months we will have our chair brochure
completed, and I will see that you get a copy.

Thank you for your interest.

Sincerely,

Charles B. Raaberg
Director of Development

CBR:mb
Enclosures

Sam proposing establishment of the 1939 Club Chair on Holocaust
studies at UCLA, April, 1997

Sam (on right) presenting a check to Chancellor
Charles Young (on left) of UCLA , for the
establishment of the 1939 Club Chair.
Picture taken November 5, 1978.

UNIVERSITY OF CALIFORNIA, LOS ANGELES

BERKELEY · DAVIS · IRVINE · LOS ANGELES · RIVERSIDE · SAN DIEGO · SAN FRANCISCO   SANTA BARBARA · SANTA CRUZ

OFFICE OF THE CHANCELLOR
LOS ANGELES, CALIFORNIA 90024

July 24, 1978

Dr. Samuel Goetz
9200 West Pico Boulevard
Los Angeles, California 90035

Dear Dr. Goetz:

I have been following with interest the progress that The 1939 Club is
making in their goal for establishing a chair at UCLA to study the circumstances and events surrounding the holocaust.

As you may know, endowed chairs have the highest priority for private
support at UCLA, and we have particular needs for chairs in the social
sciences and humanities areas. This fact is underscored by the reality of
very tight state budgets in the foreseeable future. The holocaust is an area
where real scholarship is needed and we believe that UCLA is the place
where this work can be done best. As you know, UCLA has already an
outstanding faculty who has done some work in this area. This endowed
chair will help focus their efforts as well as help us attract new scholars
of eminence to strengthen this program.

We at UCLA approve and applaud your efforts on our behalf. Please
accept our thanks for your help and pass our thanks on to your colleagues
who are working so hard to make this chair a reality.

Sincerely,

Charles E. Young
Chancellor

Sam receiving letter from UCLA Chancellor
Charles F. Young, 1978.

Sam at UCLA, upon opening the 1939 Club Chair on Holocaust studies.

The dedication of the 1939 Cub Chair on November 5, 1978. **From left**: Dr. Gertrude Goetz, Sam Goetz and Israeli's Ambassador Abba Eban.

Sam and his wife Gerti at the dedication of the UCLA endowed chair.

Sam being awarded UCLA's "Benefactor Award" by
Vice Chancellor Allan Charles upon establishment of
chair of Holocaust studies.

liberated concentration camp. The years between these two events were filled with a process of dehumanization, a process that had employed the resources of a modern state to destroy communities, to separate families, to destroy institutions, and to disrupt any form of normal life. This process, known by the euphemistic term of *Endlösung* (Final solution) had required a well-organized strategy of deception. The transports of victims destined for destruction were often labeled as transports of people destined to work in the "East." The gas chambers in the extermination camps were called the "bath" or "shower rooms." Could it be that now, in the seventies, this strategy of deception and distortion was suddenly bearing fruit?

Publications by revisionist historians and pseudo-scientists began to convince readers that very few people had in fact perished in the camps, and that those Jews who did die had done so from natural causes. This "hoax of the six million" triggered a surge of partially suppressed memories. How could anyone try to deny us the reality of our experience of these terrible events? The images that frequently flashed before my eyes were of the faces of family and friends during the moments of separation. We were the witnesses of what had happened to the others. I had watched as small children were torn away from their parents, just as I had been torn away from my own parents, never to see them again.

The "hoax of the six million" triggered anger, frustration, and a need to respond. But how could I respond? In January 1977 I made an inquiry at the University of California to see what it would cost to fund an academic chair in the department of history on the Holocaust. Angered by the stream of publications revising the actual historical facts of the Holocaust, I helped raise funds to establish this educational response at UCLA.

But the denial of the Holocaust also triggered a need for a personal response. I began to organize fellow Holocaust survivors to share their experiences on videotape at UCLA. Reluctantly at first, survivors began to share their stories with their families as well as with other members of their communities. It was difficult to share the pain and the sorrows of the war years in front of strangers and a camera. I sat in a little room with a monitor and a camera and listened to my fellow survivors. The stories were so familiar: life in the ghettos, being separated from loved ones, deportation and the final experiences in the concentration camps. I saw the anguished faces as the stories were told, the tears streaming down the survivors' faces, and the moments in which memories were overwhelmed by emotions and the story-telling came to an abrupt stop.

I began again to reflect on my own story. How do you compress six years of your life into one hour on videotape? Those six years were so different from any American teenager's life. I imagined myself as an eleven year old boy growing up in the United States and the stages I would have gone through: the soda fountain, my first girlfriend and the slow but determined progress through high school where I felt sure I would have developed close and lasting friendships. Two worlds separated by an ocean. But my fantasies were suddenly interrupted. The monitor showed the face of a survivor breaking down in tears. The interview was stopped. Fifty-seven survivor stories were placed on the shelves of the UCLA library. Perhaps someday a student would use them to peer into the dark episode of Nazi-dominated Europe.

On November 12, 1980, I helped affix a memorial plaque to the pillars of Bunche Hall at UCLA. It reads:

UCLA Endowed Chair the '1939 Club' a professorship dedicated to the study of the Holocaust and its significance within the broader historical and intellectual context, and in eternal memory to the six million Jews—men, women and children who perished, to the millions of other faiths who lost their lives. And to all those who stood up for human rights. So that it will never happen again.

The memorial plaque filled a void. It compensated for the

inability of survivors like myself to place memorial stones on the graves of our loved ones. It became a collective memorial for the six million, including my own family.

For the first time in forty-four years I returned to Poland, accompanied by my wife Gerti, and our friends Ora and Arnie Band, in June 1985. The house on Pilsudski Street where I had lived from 1934 until 1940 looked the same. Two of my former school-mates had lived in this building—Edek Dar, who had been deport-ed to Belzec in September 1942 and Ignatz Pomerantz, who escaped with his parents to the East in 1939. It was here that in late November 1939, I had felt the cold steel of a revolver pressed against my temples by a Nazi civilian. It was from here in this building that I had seen the burning synagogue on the horizon on a cold winter night in late 1939. As I entered the four-story apart-ment building I remembered the blue tile covering the entrance hall. I climbed the stairs and on the first floor I recognized the door to my former apartment. A visible space on the door, where the name Goetz had once been, was now empty. A new generation occupied the apartment. As I left the building, I wondered if the new occupants were aware of what had happened to the previous tenants.

I left the building with mixed emotions. I went on to a park where I had spent many happy moments as a child. I recognized the bench under a weeping willow tree, where I had once sat with Tekla. Try as I might, I could find no trace of anyone who had known Tekla, who had died in 1964. I hoped to find the person who had written Tekla's letters to me (she never learned to write herself), but in vain. Unable to discover where she had been laid to rest, I could not even visit her grave and say a last farewell to her there.

The building where I had worked in 1942-43 on Goldhamera 10 was being renovated. It was here that both Tekla and I had risked our lives to talk through the window. It was here that she would bring me food, and it was here where I made my plans to escape from the ghetto. It was in this building that the Germans had organized the many workshops of the ZFH to produce items for the German army and where I witnessed the painful reunion of a Jewish father and his half-Jewish son, who had traveled from Germany to meet his father for the last time. Contained within its walls were the many sounds and emotions of people who, soon afterwards, perished in Nazi extermination camps.

As I saw the front entrance, which had not changed at all, my memory flashed back to images of uniformed Gestapo agents entering through it in 1942-'43 in order to obtain custom made items such as leather coats, boots, and sweaters made by the Jews they were sooner or later going to annihilate. It was also through this gate I would sneak out to the street in early 1943 to obtain the Nazi propaganda newspaper the *Krakauer Zeitung*, in which I learned about the German defeat at Stalingrad in February of that year.

My last stop in Tarnow was the little house on Urwana Street where I had lived with my parents from 1940 to June 15, 1942. Through my window I had watched as the German trains carried troops, tanks, and other war materiel to the East and later returned with damaged tanks and planes. They were exciting sights for a child who did not know what the near future would bring. It was here the three SS men came to pick me up on June 11, 1942. It was on this street the SS men with the horse-drawn buggy picked up my father for the first time. And it was here, at 6 P.M. on June 15, 1942, I saw the train carrying several thousand Jews from Tarnow, among them my parents, leaving for the East. Forty-three years later not much had changed on this street. The trees had grown a little higher, some houses had changed color, but most of all, the Jews of Tarnow had vanished forever.

Standing outside the old apartment on Urwana Street, I noticed a man watching me with curiosity from the window of the house next door. He asked me what I was looking for, recognizing from my clothes perhaps that I was not a local resident. I told him what I was doing there and he realized he knew me; he was the son of the railway worker who had owned the house when we lived there. He had been seventeen years old at the time and not a very pleasant youth, but now he invited us into his home and we spent two hours talking with him. It was a moving experience to meet up with this person from my past life in Tarnow.

He told us his father had been arrested by the Gestapo in 1944 for letting a Jew live in the house and that the Jew had been caught and shot later that same year. At one point he left the room and returned with some photo albums in his hand. My heart jumped: could they be of my family? But they turned out to have belonged to the Wahl family, our Jewish neighbors. This man also told us something we had never heard about the deportations: on September 4, 1943, while the ghetto was being liquidated, a group of Jews had barricaded themselves off at the railway station and had resisted being deported. They must have known it was a help-less fight, but chose to die fighting there in Tarnow, rather than in the gas chambers of Belzec. The only witnesses to their heroic strug-gle were members of the Polish underground who had watched from a distance.

I left the city of my birth with mixed feelings. The houses and the streets reminded me of my childhood, the worry-free days, and the innocence of early youth. Yet, at the same time, the images of the terrible days of the Nazi occupation intruded upon these memories.

The Austrian plane left the Warsaw airport and landed one hour later in Vienna. As we landed at the airport I felt a sense of relief. Gone were the soldiers with machine guns and the gloomy, depressing feeling that pervaded Warsaw. The Austrian capital, with its stores full of attractively displayed merchandise and food items, provided a vivid contrast to the cities of Poland. As I walked by the Bristol Hotel, next to the Opera, I recalled the postcard from my father, sent in July 1938 to my summer camp in Muszyna in the mountains of southern Poland. My father had been staying in the Bristol Hotel at that time, and now I felt an urgent desire to request the guest book of that July in order to see his signature. But I restrained myself, reasoning that the hotel guest book from 1938 would no longer exist. I returned to Los Angeles. My visit to Poland had rekindled so many memories of the distant past.

Three years later I returned with Gerti to Poland to visit Belzec. The date was June 15, 1988; my parents had arrived at Belzec on June 15, 1942. Belzec is a small village in a very remote and isolated section of southeastern Poland, very close to the Ukrainian border. In March 1942, the Nazis established an extermination camp in this desolate region of occupied Poland. The camp was in operation from March 1942 until the end of December 1942. In June 1942, I had learned from my Polish neighbor that the trains transporting Jews from Tarnow were destined for Belzec. Now I stood in front of a small iron gate reading a sign posted in several languages: "Six hundred thousand Jews perished on these grounds, killed by the Germans during their occupation of Poland." I entered through the gate; the skies were gray, the air was cold. I approached the little sculpture in the center of the camp. It was of a mother holding a small child, the face of desperation. I scooped up a handful of the sandy soil, and fragments of human bone appeared in my hand. It was here my parents, my aunts, my uncles and cousins, as well as most of my classmates, had met their terrible deaths. It was here I had been destined to die, saved only by a blue Nazi swastika rubber stamp on my ID card, and then again a few months later by another stamp in green ink.

I stood looking at this desolate place: there were no visitors, no monuments, just a small parcel of land surrounded by trees. It was a forgotten place with no living survivors to tell the story of what had happened here—to tell of the barracks, the bath-house with the diesel engine attached to it, the bestial behavior of the SS guards and the dreadful deaths inflicted on the innocent Jewish men, women, and children. For a moment I thought about my parents, so young and so naive, doing business in Germany, speaking the language, and yet unable to anticipate the dreadful future. I left Belzec feeling depressed, drained, and empty. I had finally seen it, the graveyard of my family, my friends and so many others. It was only by a fluke that my own life had not ended there.

In June 1989, the UCLA Alumni Association honored me with its Community Service Award. I was given a few minutes to share my impressions about the meaning of the award in front of a thousand alumni. I began to speak. I told the audience that during the Second World War my parents had risked my life to enable me to continue my education. I spoke about the thrill of learning I had experienced here at the university. The once distant dream of being free, of leading a normal life and attending a university, had become a reality. The audience of UCLA alumni, young and old, listened. Could they have comprehended what I really meant?

On April 1993, a cold and rainy day, I sat in front of the newly dedicated Holocaust Museum in Washington. The clouds and the rain provided a fitting ambience of gloom that corresponded to the sorrowful past to which the museum is dedicated. President Clinton addressed the assembled audience. For the many survivors present it was a moment of validation, as the president recounted the history of the Holocaust and the experiences of those who had been the victims of the Nazis.

Two years later, at the rotunda in the Capitol building in Washington DC, my name was called and I was asked to light one of six candles in memory of the six million Jews who perished. I joined hands with an American GI who, fifty years ago, had entered the Nazi concentration camp at Dachau as a liberator. For a moment

SOUL SURVIVOR
Samuel Goetz '55

Meeting Sam Goetz, you'd never guess the horrors he endured as a child. The soft-spoken optometrist is a cheerful soul with a successful practice in West Los Angeles and several community service awards under his belt, including a 1989 UCLA Alumni Award for Excellence.

But at age 11, Goetz saw his birthplace of Tarnow, Poland, occupied by Nazi soldiers. He lost his parents, aunts, uncles and grandparents when he was 14 and spent three years in concentration camps. Finally, in 1945, Goetz was liberated from the Mauthausen/Ebensee camp by the U.S. Army.

The teenager lived in a displaced persons' camp in Italy, where he met his future wife, Gertrude. In 1949, he arrived in New York to stay with relatives, then a year later joined Gertrude in California. After attending Los Angeles City College at night, Goetz transferred to UCLA.

"When I came to this country and to UCLA, I was like a blank page that suddenly became filled with information," Goetz recalls. "I was so anxious and hungry for knowledge."

Goetz's ties to UCLA did not end after his graduation from the School of Public Health in 1955. In the early '60s, he served as president of the 1939 Club and initiated the drive to endow the UCLA "1939 Club" Chair in Holocaust Studies — the first such chair in the United States, now held permanently by Professor Saul Friedlander.

In fact, his entire family — wife Gertrude, son Joseph and daughter Genie — all are UCLA graduates.

Beyond UCLA, Goetz is chair of the Martyrs Memorial Museum of the Holocaust, located on the ground floor of the Jewish Federation Building in Los Angeles. He also serves on the content committee for the U.S. Holocaust Memorial Museum in Washington, D.C., which opened last April.

"My wife and I were invited by President Clinton to the opening at the White House," says Goetz. "It was a nice reception except that it was in a tent, it was pouring and it was freezing! They said it was one of the coldest Aprils in Washington.

"But there were many dignitaries there, the vice president as well as the presidents of several countries," he continues with a smile. "It was one of those memorable days."

Sam's story appears in UCLA magazine in winter, 1994—picture taken when Sam received the alumni award.

1980
United States
Holocaust Memorial Council

United States Holocaust Memorial Council

Chairman

September 9, 1987

Mr. Samuel Goetz
9337 Sawyer
Los Angeles, California 90035

Dear Mr. Goetz:

By virtue of the authority vested in me as Chairman of the U.S. Holocaust Memorial Council (PL 96-388, 10/7/80), it is my pleasure to appoint you as a member of the Content Committee. The Terms of Reference for this committee, as reviewed by the Executive Committee and approved on July 29, are enclosed. I know you'll find this work rewarding in the furtherance of the mandate and goals of the Council.

I am reminded by the staff that I must inform non-Council members that we are prohibited by law (PL 99-190, Section 101(d)) from providing compensation, travel or per diem to non-Council members serving on Council committees. Hopefully this will not pose a burden to you, and we are thus relying upon your dedication and commitment to this historic project in asking you to serve.

Thank you in advance for your service to this important committee.

Sincerely,

Harvey M. Meyerhoff

Enclosure

Sam's appointment to member of the content committee of
U.S Holocaust Memorial Museum.

Sam and Gerti's invitation to the White House, April 21, 1993.

Left to right: Bill Lowenberg, Vice Chair of the U.S. Holocaust Memorial Council; Sam Goetz the author, and California Governor Pete Wilson, at reception honoring the opening of the United States Holocaust Memorial Museum, April, 1993.

Sam lighting a memorial candle in the U.S Capitol Rotunda, on Days of Remeberence.

Sam at the United States Holocaust Memorial Museum cornerstone dedication, Washington D.C., October 5, 1988.

Dr. Sam Goetz with Jan Kanski at L.A. Museum of the Holocaust honoring Jan Kanski.

Goetz to head Martyrs' Memorial

Optometrist **Sam Goetz** has been elected to a two-year term as chair of the Martyrs' Memorial and Museum of the Holocaust, located on the ground floor of the Jewish Community Building, 6505 Wilshire Blvd. in Los Angeles. He succeeds **Jack I. Saltzberg.**

Goetz was 11 when the nazis occupied his birthplace of Tarnow, Poland. He lost his parents when he was 14 and spent three years in concentration camps. He was liberated at Mauthausen/Ebensee.

Following his liberation, he lived in a displaced persons camp in Italy. In 1950, he graduated from UCLA with a degree in public health and went on to earn a doctor of optometry degree from the Southern California School of Optometry.

He has been actively involved in Holocaust education and survivor affairs as president of the 1939 Club, through the Anti-Defamation League of B'nai B'rith, the United States Holocaust

SAM GOETZ

Memorial Council and as a member of the Martyrs Memorial executive committee. Dr. Goetz was instrumental in establishing the first chair of Holocaust Studies in the United States at UCLA.

United States Holocaust Memorial Museum Cornerstone
Dedication, Washington D.C., Wednesday, October 5, 1988.
Left to right: Unknown, Jack Tramiel (Sunnyvale, CA), Dr. Sam
Goetz (L.A.), Fred Diament (L.A.), Mrs. Helen Tramiel
(Sunnyvale, CA), Unknown.

I saw the American tank rolling through the gate of the Mauthausen-Ebensee concentration camp fifty years ago and the hollow faces of the emaciated inmates who kissed the hands of an American soldier. The ceremony ended and the honor guard left, bearing the flags of the army units which had liberated the concentration camps.

Early in the morning of October 18, 1995, I boarded a United Airlines flight to Munich. Several months previously I had received an invitation via the German consulate in Los Angeles to go to Germany and visit the Holocaust memorials there. The trip was sponsored by the Inter Nationes agency and funded by the German foreign office. Along with seven other US invitees I arrived in Munich the next day. Several hours later I was on my way to the former Dachau concentration camp. As the only member of the US group who had spent three years in Nazi concentration camps, my great concern was whether I would be able to separate my past from the present. I did not want to be overwhelmed by the past. The sight of the barbed wire, the guard towers, the barracks, the crematoria, and the photo exhibits of the SS guards' cruelty, were bound to evoke a strong emotional response in me. I determined to deaden my emotions as I had done during the war when, beset by cruelty, starvation, beatings, hangings, shootings, and separations from loved ones, I had become numb to my surroundings. Thus, when I entered Dachau, my emotions had been frozen but this time with full awareness.

The grounds of the former concentration camp were spotless. Large numbers of visitors, many from German schools, could be seen crisscrossing the grounds. The museum director, Barbara Distel, explained about life in the camp, the organization of the SS, and the punishments. This was my official welcome to Germany. Three hours away lay the concentration camp from which I had emerged, emaciated, starved, clad in blue-striped pajamas, without shoes, but with a will to live. Did I need this introduction to camp life? Should I have interrupted the museum director in order to give her my first-hand account? When I returned to my hotel my emotions were still on ice but ready to melt.

The following morning I visited the Luitpold Gymnasium in Munich. I was curious to hear what was taught about the fate of the Jews and the extermination camps. I was given a copy of the senior class history book and then joined the principal, the history teacher, and a group of students ranging in age from sixteen to seventeen. We talked about the life of Jews in Nazi Germany. I finally told them that I had been sixteen when I was liberated from a place only three hours away from Munich. The students asked questions, wanting to know about life in a concentration camp. How had I survived? I had no answer. Was it faith, destiny, chance? A million and a half-Jewish children perished. I told them that most of my classmates were killed. The students seemed subdued. Was I the first survivor they had met? I left the classroom thinking about my schoolmates, Abras, Moniek, Tulek, and Sianka.

On Sunday morning I visited the Muhltal valley. This is the area leading to the communities of Gauting and Seeshaupt where a chain of memorial sites was built to commemorate the death march from the Dachau concentration camp. In April 1945, when the US forces were approaching, the mostly Jewish camp inmates were forced to march through these communities. The majority of them perished. When the American armies liberated this area, the Jews were buried in the cemetery at Gauting. Now, as I viewed the memorials along the roadside, I recalled how, in January 1945, I marched for two weeks in the southern part of Silesia, south of the then German city of Breslau. I thought of my friend Willy, from Hungary, who was with me on that death march but who did not survive.

The following day, I met with a group of students from the University of Bonn. The students were in their early twenties, studying economics, history, and finance. They spoke good English. I asked them what they knew about the events of World War II, particularly what they had learned from their own families. Most of them admitted their grandparents were reluctant to talk about the war with them.

On Wednesday, October 25, I sat in a large room used in the past by the Gestapo concentration camps' administration and which was now Sachsenhausen Memorial. I listened as the memorial's director narrated the history of the Sachsenhausen concentration camp, located about forty-five minutes north of Berlin by car and which had opened in 1936. The windows in the room were open. Suddenly there was the sound of dogs barking, exactly like the barking of the German shepherd dogs used by the SS guards years ago. For a moment I found myself transported back to the SS roundups as they liquidated the Tarnow ghetto. The director excused himself, explaining that the German police received training in crowd control on the campgrounds. I was overcome by an eerie feeling.

A few hours later I visited the site of the former Ravensbruck women's concentration camp. I inspected the "bunker" where the female inmates were punished. In one room were records of the inmates' arrivals. Linda Hurwitz, a member or our group found the names of her aunt and her cousin and the date of their arrival from the Lodz ghetto in November 1944. Her face paled as she read the names. I helped her out of the room.

Later in the evening I visited the site of the former Gestapo headquarters in Berlin. All that remained of them was located in what was once the cellar of the building and which had now been converted into a temporary museum called "The Topography of Terror." There were documents and photos on display. I saw several photos of high-ranking Gestapo officials responsible for the killing of Jews, I read their applications to join the Nazi Party and followed their rise in the Party. They looked so ordinary in plain clothes and yet so menacing in uniform. As I left the site of the building at Prinz Albrecht Strasse, which from 1933 to 1945 had been the "House of Terror," I wondered what had made them commit their inhuman acts without remorse or pity, even for small children.

The next day I went to the Wannsee conference house, located on Wannsee lake. In January 1942 the villa served as the site where Reinhard Heydrich informed the various functionaries and ministries of the German Reich about the decision to annihilate the Jews of Europe. This "Final Solution" put in motion all the resources of the Nazi state to kill the Jews by the modern technique of gassing. I entered the room where large photos of those who attended the conference were on exhibit and where, on a large table, copies of the documents were displayed. The room gave me an uneasy feeling. In January 1942 I was living with my parents. The winter in occupied Poland was very harsh, and the new year was an uncertain one for the Jews, with the victorious German armies occupying most of Europe. I had just turned thirteen, and was unaware that some four hundred miles to the west, in a villa beside a picturesque lake in Berlin, my family's fate had been sealed.

I left the Wannsee villa and looked out onto the lake with January 1942 weighing heavily on my mind. I thought of how the Jews of Tarnow were deprived of their basic rights, confined to a ghetto with little food, and staples like bread, sugar, and milk only available on the black market. Most people had no money to buy them and therefore went hungry or even starved. Still, a measure of hope had prevailed in the ghetto. Perhaps the war would end some day soon; perhaps we would survive.

I made my way to the newly rebuilt Oranienburger Strasse synagogue in Berlin. It was partially burned on November 8, 1938 and finally reopened in May 1995. Now heavily guarded, the tall structure, with its large gilded cupola, could be seen from a great